Young**Writers** 2005 POETRY COMPETITION

Playground Poets

Let your...

D0735394

ode

limerick haiku

rhyme

ballad

Surrey

Edited by Steve Twelvetree

 Young**Writers**

First published in Great Britain in 2005 by:
Young Writers
Remus House
Coltsfoot Drive
Peterborough
PE2 9JX
Telephone: 01733 890066
Website: www.youngwriters.co.uk

All Rights Reserved

© Copyright Contributors 2005

SB ISBN 1 84602 152 9

Foreword

Young Writers was established in 1991 and has been passionately devoted to the promotion of reading and writing in children and young adults ever since. The quest continues today. Young Writers remains as committed to the fostering of burgeoning poetic and literary talent as ever.

This year's Young Writers competition has proven as vibrant and dynamic as ever and we are delighted to present a showcase of the best poetry from across the UK. Each poem has been carefully selected from a wealth of *Playground Poets* entries before ultimately being published in this, our thirteenth primary school poetry series.

Once again, we have been supremely impressed by the overall high quality of the entries we have received. The imagination, energy and creativity which has gone into each young writer's entry made choosing the best poems a challenging and often difficult but ultimately hugely rewarding task - the general high standard of the work submitted amply vindicating this opportunity to bring their poetry to a larger appreciative audience.

We sincerely hope you are pleased with our final selection and that you will enjoy *Playground Poets Surrey* for many years to come.

Contents

Faris Hussein (8)	22
Gregory Hodgson (8)	22
Adam Cresswell (9)	23
Maddie Wackett (8)	23
Bethany Howard (8)	24
Adam Ward (8)	25
Bryony Howard (11)	25
Scarlett Brice-Adams (8)	26
Rebecca Barnes (8)	27
Tommy Ellison (9)	28
Rebecca Mullett (9)	28
Harvey Godden (8)	29
Jonathan Griffiths (10)	29
Joshua Morris (9)	30
Alexander Wenk (9)	31
Jamie Braysher (8)	32
Drew Rutherford (8)	32
Caroline Matthews (8)	33
Mariel Killoughery (8)	33
Dominic Krajewski (8)	34
Jonathan Pearson (11)	35
Fraser Watt (8)	35
Lizzie Stevenson (9)	36
Elizabeth Diggins (11)	36
Tom Shopland	37
Camilla Shopland (11)	37
Eliott Strutt (10)	38
Jamie Beard (11)	38
Harry Ellison (9)	39
Olivia Pipe (8)	39
Jessica Frise (9)	40
Lizzie Raye (7)	40
Rachel Grimstone (9)	41
Alice Diggins (11)	42
Jack Deith (12)	43
David Ratcliff (13)	44
Samuel Slater (7)	44
Amy Levine (7)	45
Elizabeth Garrett (13)	46
Ilsa Forsberg (12)	47
Isabella Sturdy (9)	47
Sebastien Carpenter (7)	48

Aldro School

Beacon Hill Primary School

Laura Egan (8)	77
Elliott Baldwin (8)	77
Siobhan Collman (8)	78
Hollie Lacey (9)	79
Jack Cooper (8)	80
Alex Doar (9)	80
Emma Pocock (9)	81
Jade O'Brien (9)	81
Sam Jefferies (9)	82
Emily Pringle (8)	83
Vicky Mehta (8)	84
Megan Witherington (9)	85
Luke Lorimer (9)	86
Mercedes Lock (9)	87
Oliver Wilkinson (9)	87
Sarah Mayson (9)	88
Tom Newman (8)	89

Cranmer Primary School

Gabrielle Thomas (8)	90
Ammar Haque (7)	90
Emily Potter (8)	91
Ryan Rae-Daniel (7)	91
Chloe Chapman (7)	92
Reece Owen-White (7)	92
Kelly Wilson (7)	93
John McCoy (8)	93
Andrew Lyndon (8)	94
Milo Mitchell (7)	94
Sarah Mepham (7)	95
Robyn Milton (7)	95
Paige Smith (7)	96
Anisa Khatun (8)	96
Clement Olutola (8)	97
Liam Hill (8)	97
Romelo Sinclair (8)	97
Leah Green (8)	98
Natalie Ashen (8)	98
Thomas Owen (8)	99
Okubea Thompson (8)	99

Furzefield Primary School

Adam Baker (11)	100
Laura Jones (10)	100
Joel Babu (10)	101
Jazmine Parker (10)	101
Hannah Glasgow (10)	102
Farida Pashi (10)	102
Stephanie Cole (11)	103
Lewis O'Callaghan (11)	103
Shaun Bowie (11)	104
Tommy Bauldry (11)	104
Ben Grogan (10)	105
Lejla Palmer (11)	105
Daniel Giannetta (9)	106
Ryan Oldridge (10)	106
Rachael Scarsbrook (10)	107
Andrew Salmon (11)	107
Karina Saul (10)	108
Hannah Banks (10)	109
Jasmin Saul (9)	109
Sophie O'Neill (10)	110
Seamus Brannagan (9)	110
Mukaoso Agwuegbo (10)	111
Ben Murphy (11)	111
Peter Rook (11)	112

Grand Avenue Primary School

Lauren Godin (9)	112
Amir Patel (9)	113
Emma Mills (10)	113
Owen Cain (10)	114
Roxanne Mehdizadeh (9)	115
Joy Nunn (10)	116
Zhuohan Li (10)	117
Kiran Jabbal (9)	117
Samuel Liles (9)	118
Samantha West (9)	118
Fiona Johnstone (9)	119
Peter Clarke (9)	119
Nishalini Ravindran (9)	120
Sam Presland (10)	121

Andrew Callam (8)   143
Stephanie Ockwell (9)   143
Lauren Trout (9)   144
Nekkita Hollett (8)   144
Samantha Ray (8)   145
Roxann Johnson (11)   145
Kane Lawe (9)   146
Danielle Addison (9)   146
Anna-Marie Hart (9)   147
Anthony Young (9)   147
Atlanta Gunstone (8)   148
Klavel Millanaise (8)   148
Jobi Freeman-Lampard (9)   149
Adam Field (9)   149
Jessica Mothersole (9)   150
Alexis Loizou (8)   150
Daniel Peter Bennet-Williams (8)   150
Jonathan Mollah (8)   151
Kirsty Brooks (8)   151
Victor Dokubo (8)   151
Katharine Semple (7)   152
Travis Jones (8)   152

Mytchett Primary School
Kayleigh Bennett (11)   153
Jodie Stevens (11)   153
Oliver Surey (11)   154
David Morgan (11)   154
Francesca Reah (10)   155
Lucy Smith (10)   155
Peter Hammond (10)   156
William Smith (11)   156
Andrew Lockwood (11)   157
Felipe Paz-Howlett (11)   157
Sean Ratcliffe (11)   158
Daniela Campitelli (11)   158
Nicole Noonan (10)   159
Christian James (11)   159
Nicola Salmon (9)   160
Ryan George (11)   160
Joseph Bartlett (10)   161

Old Vicarage School

Ines Anderson (10)	184
Anna McGrane (7)	185
Louise Rogers (10)	185
Lydia Guest (10)	186
Louisa Azis (10)	186
Ellen O'Neill (9)	187
Maggie Gray (10)	187
Shaima Mirza (10)	188
Rebecca Krol (10)	189
Miranda Bowden-Doyle (10)	190
Victoria James (10)	191
Ellie Williams (10)	192
Shruti Sitaram (10)	193
Catherine Neale (11)	194
Helena Westerman (10)	195
Lucinda Barry (10)	196
Lucy Cowen (10)	197
Lucy Iremonger (9)	198

Reigate St Mary's Preparatory & Choir School

Ben Large (11)	198
Thomas Williams (11)	199
Alexander Brumwell (10)	199
Jordan Carey (10)	199
Elizabeth Boodhoo (10)	200
Aditya Gandhi (10)	200
Adam Vidler (11)	200
Hilary Stoughton (11)	201
Euan Tilling (11)	201
Zach Sullivan (10)	201
Luke Cattaneo (11)	202
Pascal Sedgwick (10)	202
Tiarnan Cotter (11)	203
George Hannigan (11)	203
Benjamin Saward (10)	203
James O'Sullivan (10)	204
Alexander Cloake (10)	204
Ryan Smith (11)	204
Samantha Cloake (10)	205
Rufus Cuthbert (10)	205
Sam Gregson (11)	205

Oliver Whippey (10)	249
William Guise (7)	249
Alexandra Moyle (9)	250
Callum McLaren (10)	250
Molly Abraham (8)	251
Sophie Lock (10)	251
Sam Haydon (10)	252
Matthew Rooke (10)	253
Rachel Williams (9)	254
George Lindley (11)	254
Daniel Saunders (8)	255
Charlotte Fagan (8)	255
Elizabeth Windridge (8)	256
Euan Hamilton (8)	256
Katy Barrett (10)	257
David Andrews (8)	258
Gus Meyer (10)	259
Haig Binnie (9)	260
Tom Morris (10)	261
Hannah Wilkinson (8)	261
Sam Clark (10)	262
Dominic Turner (8)	263
Isabel Elsey (10)	263
Gabriel Gould-Davies (9)	264
Sean Addley (9)	265
Oliver Kerr (8)	265
Max Baart (10)	266
Kitty Marryat (8)	266
Katherine Perkins (10)	267
Charlie Bramhall (9)	267
Abi Haffenden (9)	268
Georgia Paul (9)	269
Rosie Meade (10)	270
Thomas Paul (11)	270
Emily McCarthy (9)	271
Michael Stephen (9)	271
Alexandro Zaccarini (9)	272
Charlotte Morris (9)	272
Susannah Pike (8)	273
Imogen Tantam (9)	274
Ellen McLaren (8)	275
Jamie Oyebode (10)	276

The Poems

Holidays

Throughout the year,
I go to school and my parents go to work,
But we get time off to have a rest,
Which I like the best.

On holidays we have lots of fun,
And we often fly to countries where there is sun.
We visit places, eat lots of food,
And swim in the pool, which is really cool.
Sometimes we go to see my grandad and aunt on a farm in Ireland
And visit lots of friends.
I love to see the animals,
And go for long walks in the fields.
I enjoyed my winter holiday in Lapland in the snow.
Gregory and I took a reindeer ride
And the reindeer rocked from side to side.

The sad thing was it ended
And we had to go back to school
And I have to say,
That wasn't very cool.

Thomas Bradbury (9)
Aberdour School

My Hedgehog

Its wet nose is a big full stop.
The hedgehog's body is like a bed of nails,
The white tips of its prickles,
Remind me of newly fallen snow.
And the paws are like slippers.
The way it sniffs reminds me
Of a vacuum cleaner,
Ready to go
Sniffing and sucking.

James Hieber (12)
Aberdour School

Seasons

Winter is behind,
Spring is brought forward,
Snow melts in the dawn sun.
The flowers open,
To the angle of the sun.
The snowdrops hang down,
Like bells made of ice.
The tweeting in the morning
Sets the busy bees making honey
And Easter comes up.
The celebration comes,
And you look around for eggs,
In the dewy-green grass.

Spring has passed
And the hot season begins.
People off to the beach,
Carrying their heavy bags.
Swimming trunks, towels,
Suncream and picnics
Followed by hungry wasps,
Attracted by delicious smells.

Summer has gone,
And another season begins.
Autumn temperatures are low,
Making flowers and wildlife die.
Leaves fall off,
With thousands of dazzling colours.
Red! Gold! Orange!
Brown! Bronze and dark yellow!
Children crunch them
Under their feet,
Playing in them.
Animals find and store food,
For a long and cold winter.
People have fires,
To keep them warm.

Autumn has gone,
And winter begins.
Now the plants lay
Down on the ground,
Still as water,
In their dead afterlife
As there are swirling
Blizzards around,
The wildlife hibernates,
Leaving only a few birds
To cheep and wondering at their fate.
I walk out onto bitter, cold ice,
With the bare trees moving rapidly,
Like a rolling dice.

Sam Bürki (9)
Aberdour School

The Hovercraft

When you start up the engine it makes quite a sound,
But it goes over all smooth ground.
It goes over water and it goes over tiles,
As though it could go on for miles.
I will play with it for hours,
I am glad it's mine and not ours.
One brother has a boat, the other has a car,
My hovercraft is better by far.
Although it must charge for hours on end,
I will play with it for hours on end.
It glides over the floor, *oh no,*
Too late, it's out the door.

Connor Findlay (10)
Aberdour School

Make-Believe

I woke up one morning,
I could not stop yawning,
I did not know what to do.

I went to my mum,
She said, 'Hello hun,'
I still did not know what to do.

We went for a walk,
We started to talk,
As I looked down at the path.

Then I saw myself riding a bike,
And my brother going on a hike,
Then it all changed.

I say myself in the sea,
Laughing at the fish in glee,
Then it changed again.

I saw the sea going red,
Then as I got out of my head,
I saw my mum saying, 'Rest your sleepy head!'

Sophie Glaas (11)
Aberdour School

The Moon

The moon shines at night,
The moon shines at day
The moon is the one that shines every day.

The moon shines every month, except for May.
The moon, the moon, oh isn't it lovely?

The moon shines on the sea
The moon shines on the snow,
Love the moon don't you know?

Zara Patel (7)
Aberdour School

My Elephant Friend

I have a small grey elephant in my bed.
I cuddle him at night when I go to sleep.
I dream of Africa in my head,
Where the elephants splash about in the deep
Of the waterhole under the trees.
I found a friend, a little elephant calf,
With small grey ears and a long grey snout.
He rolls around in the mud of his bath,
And on the rocks the hyenas shout,
'Cause they're trying to steal the honey from the bees.
A family of warthogs trot onto the sand
Their tails up straight as they go for a drink.
They must have the sharpest tusks in the land
But boy, oh boy, they sure do stink!
Then I wake up with a jump and a sneeze.

Nicholas Taffinder (7)
Aberdour School

Poker

I deal the cards fast and swift,
My opponent's mouth begins to lift.
I take a glance,
And have a fifty-fifty chance.
Ace, king, queen, jack in my hand,
If I can't win, no one can.

The last card dealt out,
'Yes,' I give a shout,
It's the card I need without a doubt.
Now I call, he has a pair,
I could have beaten it with my underwear.
Anyway, there is no rush,
I have beaten you with a royal flush.

Christopher Huber (10)
Aberdour School

My Pet

(My pet cat)

My pet cat runs around
Without even a sound.
Her little feet pounce about,
Running up and down the couch.

When we say, 'Dinner time'
My cat comes and starts to whine.
When we put her bowl on the floor,
She puts her head in and fishes it out with her paw.

Then when she's finished she licks her fur,
When she's done she starts to purr.
Then she climbs upon my lap,
She walks around going tap, tap, tap.

It's so quiet when she's sleeping,
On my lap not even peeking.
Then when she's woken she goes outside
And climbs on my slide.

Hannah Pipe (11)
Aberdour School

My Puppy

I have a new puppy called Candy,
She is fluffy and light brown.
Her nose is small and soft,
She likes cuddling me in my bed,
She is friendly to people.
She likes jumping in puddles in the rain with her friends
And gets dirty paws.
She likes to chew on my clothes and my teddy bears.
She hides when she is frightened
Even though she is naughty, she is my best friend.

Riya Patel (7)
Aberdour School

Dubai With My Eyes Shut

I am lying on my sunbed on a beach in Dubai,
Listening to all the sounds happening nearby.
The spinning blades of a helicopter,
The splashing of the sea,
People chattering around me.

I am standing in the sea on a beach in Dubai
Feeling all the things that are nearby,
The rough gritty sand all between my toes,
The very warm water tickling my knees,
The hot sun blazing down is cosy.

I am sitting in a café on a beach in Dubai,
Breathing in the different smells nearby
The seawater smells of fish and salt
The flowers of a girl's perfume is nice
And the food smells of delicious spice.

Eleanor Musgrove (7)
Aberdour School

My Pet

Buster is my bulldog
He is my best friend,
He loves me and I love him.

When I'm sad he makes me glad,
Buster trots around the room like a horse,
He snores like a lion's growl all night long,
In the morning he is full of delight,
At the thought of his morning walk.

Buster is my bulldog,
He is my best friend,
Buster will be with me until the very end.

Francesca Hammond (9)
Aberdour School

Seasons

Winter is cold.
Winter is frosty.
Winter is when you take a nice walk.
Winter is when you play in the snow.
But then, to your dismay, the snow will melt away.
Spring comes rolling in like the sun.
Daffodils come up and spin.
The flowers come up in praise.
The cows come into the fields to graze.
Summer is coming, and it's coming fast.
Summer is here, 'Oh boy! Oh boy!'
Boys frolic on the beach.
The sun looks like a giant peach
So take a rest.
Autumn will soon be here
Autumn is here
The leaves wither
You start to shiver
Now we must rake the leaves up
'Come on! Hurry up!
Winter will be back again.'

Daniel Fromyr (8)
Aberdour School

Holidays

H appy children swimming in the pool
O n sandy beaches, happy as can be
L aughing and shouting having fun
I n far away places, enjoying their meals
D ay after day the sun comes out and brightens up the day
A fter the sun goes down, the children go to bed.
Y early holidays are so much fun
S o I wish I was there now, dreaming of the next one.

Jacob Bailey (8)
Aberdour School

Seasons

This is spring,
The flowers start to grow.
The buds begin to bloom,
The birds cheerfully sing.

Summer is here,
Warm and sunny.
The lazy days get longer,
It's the end of a hard school year.

Autumn is coming,
Colourful leaves fall off the trees.
They scrunch beneath my feet,
And the busy bees stop humming.

Winter brings a white blanket of snow,
Everywhere is freezing cold.
Children like to make smiling snowmen,
The temperature is very low.

Lucy Upot (8)
Aberdour School

My Pet

My hamster lives in a cage,
He is seven months of age,
He is soft to feel
And he runs in his wheel.
He wakes at night and sleeps at day,
He needs to be healthy to play.
My hamster is very sweet,
And he has little feet.
He has very sharp claws
On the end of his paws.

James Tudor (7)
Aberdour School

Four Seasons

Spring is the season of wind, rain and sun.
The days turn longer; the spring showers fall down,
The beautiful cherry and white blossoms come out,
And the young birds make their nests up in the tallest trees.

Summer is the season of sunshine,
All the plants are out.
Warmer days, young green leaves maturing
Long grasses mowed down to the ground,
Children playing, having fun,
Summer fruits ready to eat,
Cool drinks and ice cream, what a treat.

Warm autumn, changing colours
Orange hue, red and yellow
Leaves rustling on the ground.
Fruits harvested, apples and pears
Shorter days, cooler evenings
Fireworks and bonfires out to play.

Winter snow, ice and rain,
Hats and coats, scarves and gloves, a common sight,
Central heating and coal fires alight,
Indoor games, family nights,
Children wish they could fly a kite.

Daniel Coppen (11)
Aberdour School

My Make-Believe Pet

He has the feathers of a peacock,
The talons of an eagle,
The eyes of a hawk,
Sometimes he talks . . .
He has the beak of a parrot,
He has the brain of an elephant,
The gracefulness of a swan,
He runs as fast as a cheetah.
He's my special pet and very rare,
I have the only one,
But
He can be dangerous because . . .
He's as sly as a fox,
As strong as a bear,
Even though he tries to take care,
No one else can see him,
But you can always feel his awe,
When I talk about him people say that he's a bore,
This made him run away,
Now he is no more.

Poppy Field (11)
Aberdour School

My Pet

My tortoise walks at a steady pace,
He walks to the starting place,
Where he is about to start the big race.

The race starts on the count of three,
My tortoise is off with lots of grace,
My tortoise wins the big, big race,
You should see my tortoise's face.

His shell is so shiny,
It gleams in the sun,
No wonder he won,
It was, oh, just so much fun.

Megan Brockman (9)
Aberdour School

Seasons

Spring is when flowers grow big and tall,
Spring is when blossom decorates the maple,
Spring is when eggs appear from the Easter bunny.

Summer is when it's warm and sunny,
Summer is when busy bees take flight and make lots of honey,
Summer is when children run around and are funny.

Autumn is when the leaves turn to red and brown,
Autumn is when the conkers fall to the ground,
Autumn is when the smell of burning fills the air around.

Winter is when the trees are dark and bare,
Winter is when the snowflakes fall silently from the air,
Winter is when Christmas stockings are filled with care.

Thomas Childs (8)
Aberdour School

Seasons

When it comes to winter, the days get shorter.
When it comes to spring, baby animals are born.
When it comes to summer, farmers grow their crops.
When it comes to autumn, leaves fall off the trees.

When it comes to winter again, you put your gloves and hats on.
When it comes to spring again, the tulips and daffodils grow.
When it comes to summer again, children play on the beaches.
When it comes to autumn again, you go to Bonfire Nights.

Round and round the seasons go.
Don't forget the ice creams fall in the snow.

Tom Beard (7)
Aberdour School

Seasons

Little baby animals like lambs and rabbits start being born.
Snowdrops, daffodils and crocuses start popping up from the ground.
Birds come back from the south to make nests and tweeting noises.

It's summer; we are going to the beach,
Making sandcastles and swimming in the sea
And eating lots of ice creams.

Tweeting birds in the trees thinking about flying south for the winter
Falling leaves on the ground,
Children playing and making noisy sounds
Children jumping in leaves,
Orange, red and yellow
Squirrels hide their nuts for the long winter ahead.

Snowy leaves, it's very cold and snow is falling down!
In the morning, frosty grass
Put on your hat, gloves and scarves.
Let's go outside on our sledges!

Lilybeth Bürki (8)
Aberdour School

My Pets

I have a cat called Snowball, he is black and white,
I have a dog called Jazz, she is colourful and bright.
I have a guinea pig called Norbet, he is blue and very light
Oops, what a mistake!

I have a horse called Rupert, he is small and a bay
I have a rat called Pat, she comes out on a sunny day,
I have a spider called Ben, he is pink and grey.
Too many pets
So what can I say?
Oops, what a mistake!

Dominique Pearce (10)
Aberdour School

Friends!

I have lots of friends.
Some like to run,
Some like to sit in the sun.
Some like to play netball,
While others like to sit in the hall.

Some of my friends are funny,
Some of them bounce around like a bunny.
Some of them think they are beautiful,
Some of them are quite wilful.

Together we like to play football,
And also a game of netball.
So boys *beware,*
Come and play against us if you dare!

When times are good, when times are bad,
My friends are there for me, even when I'm sad.
Quite a lot of friends, I'm lucky to have,
We all like to laugh and play, which really is not bad!

Róisín Monaghan (10)
Aberdour School

Friends

Friends are people who look out for each other,
They don't make fun of you.
They are loving, caring, helpful and kind,
And they make you laugh too.

They play with you and come to stay,
They cheer you up when you're down.
They keep your best secrets safe,
And they're great to be around.

They are filled with glee, as happy as can be,
They give you friendship bracelets.
They are sometimes sporty and sometimes not,
But most of all, they are great!

Lauren O'Donnell (8)
Aberdour School

Summer Is My Favourite Season!

I like summer because it is hot,
I feel I'm in a boiling pot!

I like to go to the beach,
I love to feel the heat on my feet.

I like to eat vanilla ice cream,
And when it's time I sit up and beam.

I love to go swimming in the sun,
Because it is part of summer fun.

I love to go paddling in the sea and when the big waves come,
It is time for summer fun.

It is time to go home, what a day.
But guess what Mum says?
We can come back, *hooray!*

Hannah Taylor (7)
Aberdour School

Make-Believe

I believe lots of stuff
I sometimes believe that there is pink fluff
I believe in too many things,
It even makes my head sting.
Because my memory is too small to store all the things I hear,
I even want to shed a tear.
I sometimes make-believe of planet Zog,
Named suitably as it is shaped as a frog,
My memory is a very precious asset of mine,
Because all it stores is truly divine!

Xavier Mama (10)
Aberdour School

My Favourite Thing To Do Is Draw!

I like to draw all day and night,
I do it in my dreams.
And when I wake,
I stretch and shake,
My mind's so full with art!
I sit down with my pens and draw:
Valentine's and birthday cards,
But not just any old cards . . .
Instead of the same old cake, balloons and a party hat . . .
I draw an old rake, baboons and a party cat!
People love my doodles.
I even draw poodles,
Pink, white, black and blue.
So when I broke my arm one day . . .
I'm very, very sorry to say . . .
I could not draw!
It's filled my head to bursting . . .
Boom!

Lauren Morse (8)
Aberdour School

Brother, Cat And Bat

I have a little brother
And I brought him to my mother
And I said,
'I want another little brother for a change.'

I have a little cat
And I brought him to my mother
And I said,
'I want a bat instead.'

Now I have a little brother and a bat
And they are so very fat.
I brought them to my mother
And I said,
'Can I give them both back?'

Luca Carraro (9)
Aberdour School

The Four Seasons

Winter, winter
When I think of you
I hear the winds blow,
And I dream of snow
Oh I love you so.

Spring, spring
Ting, zing,
Primroses, daffodils, bluebells bloom,
That lovely scented smell,
Oh I love you so.

Summer, summer,
Those summer smells,
I see shells
And seagulls squawking,
Oh I love you so.

Autumn, autumn,
Crack, crunch,
My feet crackle on the frosty leaves,
Red, orange, yellow, gold,
Oh I love you so.

Jessica Scholfield (10)
Aberdour School

Holidays

Holidays, holidays,
Such a refreshing type of day.
All the time you're having fun!
Stay up late and watch TV!
So everybody joins in!
Make some friends!
Have a swim!
What will your destination be?

Ramsey Lawrence (9)
Aberdour School

The Bahamas

'Hurray.' It's holiday time at last,
We're packing bags and cases.
We're flying off to have some fun
In hot and distant places.

We've packed our clothes and swimwear too.
The suncream, glasses and beach shoes.
The case is closed; we shut the front door,
There is no time left to lose.

We catch the train, we can't be late,
We're heading for our plane.
We queue and queue, the check-in's long,
I feel I'm going insane.

We fasten our belts; we're ready for take-off
The pilot talks to the crew.
The engines roar loudly, the wheels spin round,
With a *whoosh* we are into the blue.

We have just arrived at our beach-side hotel,
We can hardly wait for a dip.
There is diving, snorkelling and sandcastles to build,
And even time for a trip.

There are fishes and dolphins and turtles that swim,
There is coral and starfish and shells on the sand.
We walk to the end of the pier and back,
Whilst listening to the band.

We got tanned from the sun, we enjoyed the meals,
But now it is time to go home.
We will miss all the fun we had but,
We know next year, back here we'll roam.

Verity Beadle (9)
Aberdour School

Favourite Things

Favourite things are chocolate and sweets,
I love to eat lots of goodies and treats.
They live in a cupboard in a jar up high,
Sometimes I feel as if I'm touching the sky.

My wakeboard makes me jump and flip,
On the water I can grind and kick,
I feel so free going around the lake,
Twisting and turning in the boat's wake.

Sunny and warm, holidays I love best,
The hotels treat us as well as a guest.
Splashing and jumping in the pool,
Makes my holidays really cool.

My most favourite things in the world,
Are my family, that can't be sold!
Love, friendship and care,
Are my favourite things to share.

Ben Smith (9)
Aberdour School

Families

Families, families, families,
Mine are so great,
My dad, my mum, my brother,
We all are best mates.

Families, families, families,
We all go out together,
My dad helps me with my homework,
Because he is so clever.

Families, families, families,
The weekends are the best,
But when it comes to Mondays
Sometimes I am a pest.

Harry Holden (8)
Aberdour School

Seasons

Autumn leaves; yellow and brown,
Blow around the windswept town
Flaming red, russet, gold and emerald-green,
From the finest trees I've ever seen.

Winter freeze icicles and snow,
Little red noses seem to glow
Children in the cold all day long,
Laughing loudly and singing songs.

In spring, buds begin to show,
Lambs are born in fields, and though
The farmers are busy harvesting corn,
They still help the sheep so the lambs can be born.

Summer heat welcomed after the warm showers of spring,
Sitting outside in the long green grass, making a game of everything.
Building sandcastles, collecting shells, splashing in the waves.
Of all the seasons, I like most the long, hot summer days.

Hannah Brown (9)
Aberdour School

My Pet

My pet Scrappy is a boy's best friend.
Lots of hair; yellow and brown
He makes me happy, but makes my dad frown,
And his bark isn't a pleasant sound.
We take him for tests
And then let him rest.
Mum said he was a pest
And Dad said he wouldn't take that lark again.
When he was a puppy he weed indoors
And anyone who'd visit, my dad would say, 'Have him, he's yours.'
He's always after food and then my mum gets in a mood.
Now he's older, what a fine dog he can be
And my mum and dad are happy because he's stopped the wee.
My pet Scrappy is a boy's best friend.

Sam Stone (9)
Aberdour School

Family Tree

Number one in my family tree
Is Grandpa Kenny who's sixty-three,
Second in my family tree is Grandad Dave
Who's wedded to Nanny Val, she's my pal.
Nanny Pauline comes calling every Saturday,
She babysits to allow Mummy and Daddy to go out to play!

My daddy is thirty-eight and often comes home quite late
Andrew is his name, golf is his game.
You will always find him on the course
I would rather ride a horse!

My mummy likes to have lots of fun!
She insists that she is twenty-one!
I think this is very poor,
Because I know she is really thirty-four!

I have two sisters Faye and Ellis
I love them very much.
I would really love a brother
But Mum says that would be too much.

Max Holder (7)
Aberdour School

The Season Of Spring

Spring is the time when nature wakes up from its long winter sleep.
All the summer sports begin.
Everyone has fun and the birds start to sing.

Spring birthdays are the best in the year.
The skies are always blue and clear.
I call it my outside time.
A time to have fun and climb.

It's the time when lambs jump and sing,
My favourite time of year is spring.

Toby Kemp (7)
Aberdour School

Favourite Things

What do I like to do?
Work and play everyday.

What do I like to play?
I'd love to play on the computer everyday.

What do I like to read?
Books on Ancient Greece.

What do I like to do in the sun?
I ride my bike because it's fun.

What do I like to eat?
Sushi, crab and lobster meat.

What do I like to drink?
Fizzy drinks that aren't pink.

But what would I love most to do?
Play Halo, Halo and more Halo 2.

Faris Hussein (8)
Aberdour School

Are They True?

Fairies, witches, are they true?
Witches mix their deadly brew.
Evil chuckle, warty face,
Crooked nose and in disgrace.

Fairies, witches, are they true?
Fairy godmothers and Tinkerbell too.
Fly around all day and night,
Twinkling, perfect, shining bright.

Wizards, warlocks, are they true?
Magic spells; old and new.
Spooky noises, scary sounds,
Ghosts appearing from the ground.

Are they true?

Gregory Hodgson (8)
Aberdour School

My Pet

Eight long hairy legs,
She likes to lay a lot of eggs.
She is very small and very calm,
Until she bites a hole in your arm!

You won't be very pleased
If she gives you a nasty disease.
Her venom is very poisonous
And her web is very sticky.

To catch her isn't easy,
It could be very tricky!

She is very scary
And Heaven knows,
She is my pet tarantula
And her name is Rose!

Adam Cresswell (9)
Aberdour School

My Skiing Holiday

I go skiing every year,
It's lots of fun,
I have no fear,
There's lots of snow,
And music too,
There's lots of fun,
And things to do.
The snow is cold,
The sun is out,
Rushing down the slopes,
I scream and shout.
After ski school, me and Ben,
Would make a great big, snowy den.

Maddie Wackett (8)
Aberdour School

Seasons

A is for autumn, when the leaves fall
And the tall trees have golden leaves.
People start to put their coats on
And wear their scarves, gloves and hats.

W is for winter, when Jack Frost starts to call
And later on, snow starts to flutter from the sky.
Children make snowmen and have snowball fights!
'Hooray.' We can play outside at school
And we can have fun in the snow all day long.

S is for spring, when the daffodils grow and the dew starts to come
And lots of other flowers start to open up.
'Hooray.' We can go swimming at school in the swimming pool,
We can get into our costumes and put on our goggles
And have fun in the pool.
With a lesson every week on a Monday at two.

S is for summer, when the weather gets hot,
And the children like to have ice creams all day long!
They want to go swimming every day in the pool -
David Lloyds is really cool!
'Hooray.' It's the summer holidays, what shall we do?
Can we go to the seaside and make sandcastles
And go swimming in the sea?
I wonder if we could go snorkelling and meet all the fish
And maybe we will even see a shark or a dolphin!

Now the summer holidays are over, we are back to school,
We have to wear our uniform, which isn't very cool!
We all have to wear the same every day,
There is no change in clothing unless it's mufti day, *'Hooray!'*

This is the end of my poem on the seasons
And if you want to change it,
You have to have some good reasons!

Bethany Howard (8)
Aberdour School

Seasons

Autumn has leaves, falling off trees,
Brown and orange, falling down.
September to November, autumn stays,
Days getting shorter, summer's all gone.

Winter is cold, icy and snowy,
Woolly hats, jumpers, scarves and gloves.
Fires burning, smoke from chimneys,
December to February, cold and shivery.

Spring all bright with colourful flowers,
From March to May, in fields and farms.
Lambs are leaping everywhere,
The summer is coming, 'Hooray!'

Summer is hot, very sunny,
Summer sunshine everyday.
May to August we laze around,
In the garden and the paddling pool.

Adam Ward (8)
Aberdour School

Seasons

Right now, it's winter and not very warm
You won't be surprised to find a storm.

Springtime is here and the flowers are out,
It's getting warmer, without a doubt.

Summer is upon us and we bathe in the sun,
Summer is hot and we have so much fun.

Autumn is here and the colour is too.
And everyone knows just what to do.

Rake up the leaves in a great big pile.
Then roll around and play in them for a while.

Winter is back and so is the cold.
Another year gone, I think I'm getting old!

Bryony Howard (11)
Aberdour School

Favourite Things

My nanny has donkeys in Portugal.
She rescues them from a hospital.
They roll in the mud and sleep in the sun,
Being with them is so much fun.

Football is my favourite sport,
We usually play on a green court.
I kick the ball and hey, we score,
But I don't like it when we draw.

My mummy is very kind,
But I think she has a crazy mind.
My mummy loves me and I love her,
If she were a cat, she would *purrr!*

Milk is smooth, milk is nice,
I like mine mixed with ice.
I think milk is scrummy yummy,
I like milk in my tummy.

Daddy is my favourite man,
He supports West Ham.
He says that I'm his top girl,
And he spins me in a whirl!

Doggy brings me so much joy,
It's hard to believe he's just a soft toy.
I love him with all my heart,
I would be upset if we were apart.

Scarlett Brice-Adams (8)
Aberdour School

My Good Friend

Early every morning,
My friend is there to see,
A-stretching and a-yawning
And waiting there for me.

She always makes her breakfast
She likes her milk and tea
We shared the bacon to the last,
My friend she is so cuddly.

Early every morning,
My friend is there to see,
A-stretching and a-yawning
And waiting there for me.

With breakfast done, we start to play,
Her eyes are dim, she may be old,
Not too old to love her day
And be protected from the cold.

Early every morning
My friend is there to see,
A-stretching and a-yawning,
And waiting there for me.

You may by now already know,
But in case you haven't guessed
My friend is my cat, she'll never go,
She will always be the best.

Rebecca Barnes (8)
Aberdour School

Make-Believe

There once was a dragon, he was red.
Where did he live?
Under my bed!

There once was a dragon, his name was Roy.
Guess what?
He wasn't a toy!

There once was a dragon, fierce and frightening.
How did he move?
Like grease lightning!

There once was a dragon who was very old.
How did he fight?
Brave and bold!

There once was a dragon, all mighty and rough.
How did he die?
He flew too high!

The poor old dragon teaches us all -
The higher you fly,
The further you fall!

Tommy Ellison (9)
Aberdour School

Holidays!

I'm going on holiday, *'Hip, hip, hooray!'*
We're leaving right away at 9am today,

Is it going to be hot?
Is it going to be cold?

Are we going on the beach?
Are we going in the snow?

We might go to America and go on lots of rides,
Or we'll go to Dubai and go on lots of slides.

Will I make friends to play with every day?
I don't know but I hope I have a lovely *holiday.*

Rebecca Mullett (9)
Aberdour School

My Dogs

My dog's called Dave, he's really fun,
He's large and black and hairy,
He loves to go on long, long walks,
He's never ever scary!

He eats a great big bowl of food
In 20 seconds flat,
Because he always goes for walks,
He'll never get too fat!

Bazil is his little friend,
A Scotty dog is he,
He has big, hairy eyebrows,
And finds it hard to see!

At night Dave sits at the end of my bed,
He snores and wriggles around,
Sometimes I kick him to move him a bit,
Then he falls onto the ground!

Harvey Godden (8)
Aberdour School

My Idol

He's as fast as a cheetah
And wears a lion on his chest.
His name is Robben and Robben is the best.

He plays on the right wing,
Skilfully dribbling the ball.
He's heading up field, beware of those in goal.

He heads for the area
And then strikes the ball,
It fires from his feet, and he scores a goal!

The crowd and the team
Jump up and all cheer
And sing, 'Robben, Robben, Robben!'

Jonathan Griffiths (10)
Aberdour School

The Fwozzle

There once was a Fwozzle,
With a very big snozzle,
The colour of blueberry jam.
And for his lunch,
He liked to munch,
On a meal of blue lettuce and ham.

He has some hair,
I don't know where,
His ears are bigger than pies,
His feet are bobbly,
His knees are knobbly,
And he has seven polka-dot eyes.

He lives in a tree,
His friend is a bee,
Who likes to give him his honey.
He likes the taste,
And won't let it waste,
The extra he sells for money.

To keep himself happy,
He puts on a nappy,
Sits on the floor and cries.
The people come out,
And start to shout,
'Fwozzle needs beddy-byes.'

You now know the Fwozzle,
With the very big snozzle,
If you see him shout, 'Hello'
He'll give you a smile,
He'll wave for a while,
And then he'll ask you to go.

Joshua Morris (9)
Aberdour School

Journey To Germany

We're off to Germany,
'Hip hip hooray!'
Tunnel under the sea,
Dad snores most of the way!

Charlott's reading,
Georgi's asleep.
'Help! I need the loo.'
A stop in the lay-by,
I go for a . . .

Off we go again,
Whizz through France.
Sail past Belgium,
Dad drives soo quick!
Zoom through Holland,
Oh no! Charlott feels . . .

Out of the lay-by,
Back on the road,
Hot and sticky,
I feel my eyes close.

Suddenly stopping,
Lights go on.
Lips on my cheeks,
Booming voices in my ear.
Oma and Opa
'Hello Alex, Du bist hier.'

Alexander Wenk (9)
Aberdour School

Make-Believe My Trip To The Moon

I flew to the moon, in a beautiful balloon.
On the way, I met an angry baboon,
Who was holding a wooden spoon.
He was hairy, scary and called himself Mary.

When I got there, I had a scare.
I landed in a crater, which looked like an alligator.
I jumped up high, into the sky
And saw a woolly lamb go bouncing by.

The ground was lumpy and ever so bumpy.
Suddenly the sky lit up green, I thought,
Oh dear, what does this mean?
Then I saw him, the man in the moon.
He had a long, pointy nose and pink, stripy clothes.

He was holding a plate of toffee and a steaming mug of hot coffee.
The ground shook and started to crumble and we heard a rumble.

'Run, run,' he shouted
I ran to my balloon and jumped inside
And tried to find a place to hide.
Back down to Earth with a bump that made me jump.
Thump, thump, thump!

Jamie Braysher (8)
Aberdour School

Sometimes It's Just Make-Believe

Sometimes it's just make-believe, to see cows that climb up trees,
And what about bees with knees?
I think they're make-believe.

Sometimes it's just make-believe, to see pigs that fly up high,
And what about pies in the sky?
I think they're make-believe.

Sometimes it's just make-believe, to see dancing to rubber bands
And what about talking hands?
I think they're make-believe.

Drew Rutherford (8)
Aberdour School

A Poem About My Rabbit

I had a pet rabbit, his name was Radish,
He was white and fluffy and cute.

He hopped around my garden,
Like a little spring lamb,
Chasing around my feet.
Carrots and biscuits
Were his favourite foods,
With lots of water to drink.

I loved him so much,
But sadly he died
On one Monday afternoon.

My mum buried him
In my garden and
We said a little prayer.

I think about Radish often,
Because I really care.

Caroline Matthews (8)
Aberdour School

Friends

Friends, friends, wonderful friends,
Kind, helpful and caring,
They are never horrid and never selfish,
They never leave you behind.
They always look after you when you are ill or hurt,
And our best friend of all is God.
He never leaves you behind,
He never calls you horrid names,
He is never selfish,
And he is always there to care.
He has given us all our friends.
We should pray to God for all our friends and family.

Mariel Killoughery (8)
Aberdour School

Here Comes, There Goes Season

Here comes white Winter
A wonderful Winter's day.
World fast asleep. Silent time.
'Splat!' Snowball fights in the streets.
'Crickle, crackle, crickle.' Morozko is out to play.
There goes Winter.

Here comes emerald Spring.
A beautiful Spring's day.
Wake up! Time to grow.
Green grass, yellow daffodils.
'Tweet, tweet.' Birds singing, lambs born.
There goes Spring.

Here comes yellow Summer.
A happy Summer's day.
The sun is out - bright and hot.
Holiday time! Harvest time!
Fun for everyone.
There goes Summer.

Here comes rusty Autumn.
A miserable Autumn's day.
'Rittle, rattle.' Leaves talking.
'Splish! Splash! Splosh!' Raindrops falling.
'Rumble bumble, crash boom!' Winds blowing.
There goes Autumn.

Dominic Krajewski (8)
Aberdour School

Holidays

Holidays, holidays they're very fun,
Holidays, holidays for everyone,
Holidays, holidays in the snow,
Holidays, holidays in the sun.

Cold, hot, ice and sand,
Inside, outside, rainy and bland,
Holidays, holidays in the sand.

America, Spain, Italy,
Portugal, Greece, Australia,
Sun, snow, wind and rain,
Lots of holidays so don't complain.

Skiing, sailing and swimming,
Donkeys, camels and horses,
Snakes, lizards and cactus,
Watch out or they'll catch us.

Car, plane and boat,
Land, air and sea,
Holidays, holidays they're very fun,
Holidays, holidays for everyone.

Jonathan Pearson (11)
Aberdour School

My Pet

My pet is called Mischief,
I'm sorry to say he is a bit of a thief.
Whenever we leave food on the table,
He jumps up and eats what he is able.
He is black and white,
He is quite a sight.
I love him,
But I wouldn't say he is slim.
My big, fat, black and white cat called Mischief!

Fraser Watt (8)
Aberdour School

My Friends

My friends are cool and have style,
And the other ones with the cheeky smile.

Then there are friends like mine with kindness,
Particularly the ones who have kindness deep down in them.

My friends are funny and full of cheer,
They make me laugh when I feel fear.

On a rainy day, a sunny smile from a friend
Makes me feel good all day.

It's so boring if I'm not with my friends,
Prefer the laughing, joking, till the end of the day.

My friends are so special to me.
I'm so lucky to be me, when friends like mine
Always please!

Lizzie Stevenson (9)
Aberdour School

Make-Believe

A little noise caught my ear,
I walked further up the garden
And there the noise was again.
Then I saw a little fairy,
It climbed a branch,
And more came out.
Suddenly they started dancing,
Some were singing,
And some were prancing.
Could there really be
Fairies in the garden,
Or was it just a dream?

Elizabeth Diggins (11)
Aberdour School

Holidays

It's hard to wake up,
When the shades have been pulled shut.
This house is haunted,
It's so pathetic; it makes no sense at all.
I'm ripe with things to say,
The words rot and fall away.
What stupid poem could fix this home?
I'd read it every day.

So here's your holiday,
Hope you enjoy it this time,
You gave it all away.
It was mine.
So when you're dead and gone,
Will you remember this night twenty years on?
It's not right!

Tom Shopland
Aberdour School

Families

I wonder where we would be,
Without our family.
Our lives would be rather glum,
And we wouldn't have a shoulder to cry on.

I'm lucky to be here with my family,
It must be hard for those in the tsunami,
We've never felt the pain they're going through,
They've got it hard compared to me and you.

I feel for those who've lost loved ones,
Killed by the tsunami or violence, like guns.
So when you're angry with your family,
You shouldn't be. Be happy.

People may have more money than me,
But I have one of the best gifts of all,
All my family.

Camilla Shopland (11)
Aberdour School

Families

Family are the ones you love,
They're always there when things get tough.
They'll stand by you, through thick and thin,
Whether you lose, or whether you win.

Family are the ones who care,
No matter what, they will be there.
They'll back you up; they'll cheer you on,
You'll never look and find them gone.

Families argue and sometimes fight,
But in the end, they'll be alright,
In the end, they'll come up strong,
You know they'll never steer you wrong.

Family are people you can trust,
They'll never fade and they'll never rust.
They'll bring you up; they'll help you out,
You can look to them without a doubt.

Eliott Strutt (10)
Aberdour School

My Pet

My tiger is orange and white,
Each morning I give it some meat to bite.
It makes its way around the cage,
Its underneath is a shade of beige.
You need to wash it. It gets smelly,
Right around the body, and under the belly.

Waiting in the grass one day,
Tiger was waiting for its prey.
As I walked over the wet floor,
Tiger walked up to the door.
I love Tiger as my pet,
We have cared for each other
Since the day we met.

Jamie Beard (11)
Aberdour School

My Pets

Pets, pets, beautiful pets,
Dogs, bats and kangaroos,
'Yahoo.' They're all as beautiful as me.

Cuddly, loyal and always true,
A pet is an absolute must for you.
Outside, inside, it's always the same,
Whenever you're lonely,
Just shout out their name.

They will soon come running
And answer your call.
Dash through the kitchen,
Run down the hall
To greet you with their love and care,
Letting you know they will always be there.

Harry Ellison (9)
Aberdour School

My Pet

Her name is Nala,
She is my cat,
When I stroke her fur,
She starts to purr.
I love her playful ways,
In the garden under the trees,
I watch my cat chase the leaves.
She's at the back door, I let her in,
She leaves her wet footprints all over the floor.
She rubs against me; it must be dinner time,
I am so glad she's mine.

Olivia Pipe (8)
Aberdour School

My Idol

He's a hero.

He says that life's exciting,
He never is a bore,
He's been around for eighty years,
And was brave in the war!

He's a superstar.

He loves going on adventures,
And trying something new,
He takes me to museums,
And sometimes castles too!

He's fun.

He's old but likes to disco,
He's brilliant for his age,
He's a gold medal winner,
And should be on the stage!

But he is not famous,
He's not on TV,
He's just my grandad!

Jessica Frise (9)
Aberdour School

The Tooth Fairy

A tooth fairy is a pretty thing,
Who loves to sing
She sits on clouds above your roof,
Until you lose a baby tooth.
She flies down to your house,
As quiet as a little mouse.
She takes your tooth to a place so far away,
And turns it into a twinkling star.
In its place she leaves some money,
For you to spend on a jar of honey.

Lizzie Raye (7)
Aberdour School

The Environment

The environment is all around us,
It was a beautiful place.
Then Adam went and started
The giant human race.

We've knocked down all the trees
And stolen the honey from bees.
And now this environment place
Is a terrible disgrace.

We've been carrying on for centuries,
Maybe a millennium or two.
But we just can't seem to stop,
We need help from *you!*

Animals' homes are being destroyed
By great, big, metal machines.
Gigantic forests are felled to the last tree,
Just to make paper for you and me.
It's not just their homes; it's the animals too,
How will they live without help from you?

We've been carrying on for centuries,
Maybe a millennium or two.
But we just can't seem to stop.
We need help from *you!*

Rachel Grimstone (9)
Aberdour School

Seasons

My palm stretched out,
Reached into the sky,
A delicate snowflake falling by.
The cold windy air,
Blows briskly through my hair.

Leaves of all shapes
Fall off the trees,
Landing on the ground like coloured seas.
The autumn sun will glitter,
And the birds will start to twitter.

Springtime is here,
Birds fly through the breeze,
The flowers are open, there are buzzing bees.
The sun now shines brightly,
Making days lighter.

The summer heat
Beats down on my back,
Cool, refreshing air is what we lack.
And in this perfect weather,
I need it more than ever.

Alice Diggins (11)
Aberdour School

Seasons

As baby Spring
Crawls slowly in . . .
His touch gives life to all.
The flowers pop out,
New lambs give a shout!

Now Lady Summer
Gracefully makes a stand . . .
As she warms up the land,
From sea to sand,
Then merrily skips away.

Enter Sir Autumn
With a large stride . . .
He blows leaves away
And shortens the day -
He is a warning of winter.

Old man Winter
Enters with snow and ice unfurled,
Sweeping the world,
As he gives a chill,
People fall ill
And baby Spring
Follows in his wake once again.

Jack Deith (12)
Aberdour School

Seasons

In spring, the flowers open up,
And show their beautiful colours.
The birds start to sing,
Because it is spring.

In summer, everyone goes to the beach
And chill with their ice creams,
They get a suntan,
Because it is summer.

In autumn, the leaves start to fall
And the squirrels start to gather nuts.
Animals start to hibernate,
Because it is autumn.

In winter, the snow starts to fall.
Children have snowball fights
And build snowmen,
Because it is winter.

David Ratcliff (13)
Aberdour School

My Pet

I have a cat
That is fluffy and fat
She is a nice cat
And she purrs a lot
She is funny.

Her name is Jess
Jess brings in mice,
Which isn't very nice,
I have to grab her by the scruff,
And say, 'That's enough!'

But she's my cat
And that is that!

Samuel Slater (7)
Aberdour School

My Pet

I have a cat,
His name is Matt,
I love him very much.
He's black and white,
With eyes so bright,
His fur is soft to touch.
I take him out for walks,
Every now and then,
Through the grass he stalks,
Chasing mice again.
I stroke his fur,
I hear him purr,
I tickle behind his ears.
He rolls on his tummy,
He really is funny,
I hope we're together for years.
At the end of the day,
After a play,
He sits on the end of my bed.
He licks his paws,
And almost snores,
He's such a sleepyhead!

Amy Levine (7)
Aberdour School

My Pet

Small, cute and fluffy.
Moving the bedding, just slightly, as she breathes.
Out from the back, a little thin tail peeps out.
You often wonder why she can't always be like this,
Snuggled up, silent.
Then there's a rustling and you groan.
You know what's going to happen next.
So you make sure you're prepared.
Prepared to focus all your concentration on one thing . . .
'The gerbil.'
She shoots out of her bed, and transfers herself over to her play area.
She zooms in, on and between boxes, tubes and other fun objects.
For five minutes, you can only see mayhem.
Then suddenly you hear a loud scrabble, followed by a soft 'plop.'
You shout to the rest of the household, 'Gerbil!'
And everyone comes running, to retrieve the gerbil,
And put her back on the table.
She has another five minutes of slower fun
And then she goes home.
She is exhausted, *(and so are you)* and she soon falls asleep.
She has had her fun for the day,
And tomorrow, it will all start again.
But for the moment, she is snuggled up, silent.
Small, cute and fluffy.

Elizabeth Garrett (13)
Aberdour School

Friendship

You were always there for me,
When we were young,
We had our good times and our bad,
But you were there when I was sad.

You were always there for me,
When we were young,
You supported me through all my tears,
We comforted each other through the fears.

You were always there for me,
When we were young,
It's really sad that it had to be this way,
But it has reached its very last day.

You were always there for me,
When we were young,
Miles away can't keep us apart,
Because you'll always be in my heart.

Ilsa Forsberg (12)
Aberdour School

My Pet

My pet is a handsome cat called Toby,
But sometimes he just looks very lonely,
He looks out of the window; he looks out of the door,
He really has no friends at all.

I've got him a friend, a hamster called Ozzy,
A companion for Toby who wasn't fussy,
But as Toby watched, he wasn't amused,
In fact he was a bit confused.

Was this new pet a friend or was it a snack?
Would anyone notice if it didn't come back?'
But for now Toby and Ozzy are the best of friends,
But I'm really not sure how the story will end!

Isabella Sturdy (9)
Aberdour School

On My Head My Son!

I go to the match with my dad
I hope the game doesn't turn out sad.
The fans are waiting for the players to come
Onto the pitch to see them run.
We cheer the red and blues from the stands
For we are Crystal Palace fans!

Here comes my idol, the best of them all
Andy Johnson and I let out a call.
He turns to me and smiles and waves
It is a memory that I will save.
He's our top scorer he is the best
Running around in his red and blue vest.

The ref blows the whistle the game has begun
Johnson breaks out with a very fast run.
With his excellent footwork he scores a great goal
Our beloved Eagles are now on a roll.
The fans leap up and let out a cheer
The scent of victory is getting near.

The game is over the match is won
Eagles are the victors, with a score of 2-1.
Andy's our hero, the man of the match
For Palace he's really a very good catch.
I turned to my dad and said, 'That was fun.'
He threw me a ball and said, 'On my head my son!'

Sebastien Carpenter (7)
Aberdour School

Favourite Things

Just think of your favourite things and toys
And think of things that fill your heart with joy.
Now take your mind to a special place
And picture images that'll put a smile on your face.

There are so many things I love to do,
But enough about me, what about you?
Whether it be rockets, skiing or just laying in bed,
Which you might find to be a perfect place to rest your head.

Now let's start thinking interesting
And not think of stuff that goes ding-a-ling-ling.
If you could save anything in the world, just say the word
And we might be thinking of the thing we heard.

So come, this sounds fun, favourite things an' all,
I think we'd better have a ball.
Don't you worry; it's just an expression,
I don't mean we'd play with one outside the delicatessen.

Now this poem is reaching its end,
But whether the thought leaves your mind, it all depends.
So here we go - one, two, three,
Just think real hard and you will see.

Shahail Woodcock (13)
Aberdour School

My Idol

Here comes my idol in a limousine,
He makes all the girls want to scream.
His name is Elvis,
He shakes his pelvis.

He's the king of rock and roll
And he has a pure soul.
His music makes you move
And get into the groove.

He had songs like 'Hound Dog' and 'Blue Suede Shoes,'
But no one could argue, he was nothing but cool!
He had a shaky lip
And a belt upon his hip.

Graceland was his home,
Where he was never alone
Because his fans were nearby,
He could always hear the girls cry.

He died very fat,
But he was still a cool cat.
His legend lives on,
It lives in every song.

Brett Milotte (10)
Aberdour School

Seasons

Spring:
In the spring, the sun comes out,
Buds open and begin to sprout.
Then we have the April showers,
When all the buds turn into beautiful flowers.

Summer:
In the summer it is hot and sunny,
The bees are busy making honey.
My mum puts it on my toast
And that is what I like the most!

Autumn:
Then the leaves turn to brown
And then we know they are going to fall down
And then there is a breeze
And all the leaves fall from the trees.

Winter:
There is lots of snow upon the ground,
On the trees, hills and all around.
Children are having lots of fun in the snow
And they all have a very red glow.

Yasmin Davies-Nash (7)
Aberdour School

Make-Believe

As I sit in boring school,
I see a mighty dinosaur,
It starts to eat the teacher's car,
I turn around for even more.

An angry tiger prowling round
The hallway is a no go
The tiger turns and looks at me
But I know what it wants though.

For in my pocket I have a ball
A fluffy ball of cotton,
And if I throw it down the hall
The tiger is forgotten.

I take a sigh of sweet relief
I then go to my classroom
When suddenly out of belief
An aeroplane to Khartoum!

And if you think I'd had enough
You surely would be wrong
The pilot asked, 'You comin' Guv?'
And, yes, I hopped along.

We flew right over France and Egypt
We circled around Italy
When suddenly an engine went
And we landed in Sicily.

We took a ferry to Japan
When there we saw Godzilla
I took him out with boxing gloves
Then came the great gorilla.

I tickled him 'til kingdom come
He didn't last much longer
I saved Japan, with my tough plan
That made me feel much stronger.

I then woke up, I realised when I saw Mrs Eve,
That all that happened wasn't real
But only make-believe . . .

Alex Sawyer (11)
Aberdour School

My Pet

My furry friend
Comes wandering through
Nose in the air, tail even higher,
A superior cat in every way.

My furry friend
Sleeps on my bed,
A furry purring mass,
A pussycat perfection.

My furry friend
Never knows what to eat.
Kit-e-kat too low ranking.
For a superior cat like her.

My furry friend
Is not a friend to other furry beasts,
So generous and kind,
She brings them to me as presents.

Olly Metcalfe (10)
Aberdour School

Families

Today I was woken by my brother jumping on my bed,
So I said, 'Please stop it, Alex, you're hurting my head!'

When I went down to breakfast,
We had a cornflake fight,
My mum told me we were naughty,
And my brother pretended to bite.

He said that he was a tiger,
So I made to put him in a cage,
He started to stamp and jump about,
And roar and shout with rage.

It was just then that my dad came in,
He was in a very good mood,
Then as quick as a wink he scooped us up,
And asked, 'What's all this food?'

At once the doorbell started to ring,
I ran to open the door,
It was my cousin Jessica
She had come to play 'til four.

We went out into the garden,
We tried to make a tent,
But all the sticks kept breaking,
And my back felt really bent!

After cousin Jessica went home
I sat and thought about today,
And when Mum came in with hot chocolate,
I sighed, 'What a wonderful day.'

Families can be annoying,
They also can be quite fun,
But I love my little brother,
And I love my dad and mum!

Harriet Walsh (11)
Aberdour School

The Seasons

Winter
The winter is cold, nobody talks.
They breathe out steam, and shiver so cold.
It's dark in the morning and cold all day,
It's icy on your cars, so you scrape away.
The sirens wail and monsters roar.

Spring
It's time for spring
And the days get longer.
We all come out to clean our houses,
And we clean our windows while we're at it.
Nursery children sleep and play.
They throw blossom at each other while laughing.

Summer
The nights get shorter
It's back to normal,
The air is filled with a grassy smell.
Along the streets, the roses bloom,
Hedges are clipped and mowers drone.
Strange things grow in the strangest places.

Autumn
Children set off back to school,
With heavy bags and stiff new shoes.
The leaves are golden and they start falling to the ground,
While at the allotments there are carrots and potatoes,
To dig up and share,
The days are shrinking,
And the nights are growing.

Eleanor Wade (9)
Aberdour School

Southwold

We wake up in the morning
And get out of bed,
We have our breakfast
With toast soldiers and fried egg.

We all get dressed
It's a sunny day
We're going to the beach
Hip hip hooray!

We get our things together
Our buckets and spades
Suntan lotion
And groovy shades.

We get to the beach
All warm and sandy.
First Mum buys us some snacks
Then some cotton candy.

12 o'clock now
Time for lunch,
Now the puppets
Mr Punch.

Time for a swim
Put on my bikini
A crab in my shoe
My brother's a meany!

Time to go home now
We had so much fun
When we get home
A lovely iced bun.

Charlotte Morris (7)
Aberdour School

The Environment

I am a bird,
Flying in the sky,
At one with my environment,
From up high.

The home of many little creatures,
Many features like logs and trees,
Holes where worms and spiders live,
This is what I see.

The nationalities of the globe,
With languages combine,
To form the world I see below,
Such miraculous design.

The natural power of planet Earth,
Unstoppable catastrophes,
Hurricanes and tornadoes,
Earthquakes and the sea.

The climate and the weather
Wind and sun and rain,
Of course it's unpredictable,
And can cause us so much pain.

I am a bird,
Flying free,
At one with my environment,
But what will the future be?

Rebecca Wood (11)
Aberdour School

Make-Believe

I dreamt of candy and of sweets,
I dreamt of lots of Quality Streets,
I dreamt of lakes of chocolate bars,
And dreamt I went right up to Mars.

I dreamt of summer and of spring,
I dreamt of lots of pretty things.
I dreamt of winter and of snow
And dreamt of crystal, my birthday stone.

I dreamt of lots of coloured leaves,
I dreamt of cats and dogs and bees,
I dreamt of lots of chewing gum,
And also dreamt of bubblegum.

I dreamt I floated on a cloud
To a land I'd never ever found,
Where trees were pink and blue and white.
The sky was yellow and very bright.

I then woke up, got out of bed,
And all the dreams flew from my head,
And all the oddly coloured leaves,
I knew it all was make-believe.

Emma Ward (11)
Aberdour School

My Kitten

I have a little kitten
She's grey and fluffy and sweet
At night when I get out of the bath
She always licks my feet.

She purrs so very loudly
And rubs against my leg
When I'm watching TV
She tries to sit on my head!

She's oh so very greedy
But I don't mind at all,
For when I drop my food
She eats it off the floor.

She's friendly and she's playful
She loves her scruffy toy rat,
And when she sees it on the floor
She takes it to her mat.

My kitten is so lovely
And cuddly as can be,
That's why I love my kitten
And I think that she loves me!

Lilli Crossley (7)
Aberdour School

Animals On The Prowl

Cats are night predators,
They sleep all day,
Wanting to be stroked
Cute, cuddly creatures
But when darkness falls
They disappear into the wilds
Hunting for prey, they show no mercy.

A baby gorilla in the misty jungle
Looks like a beanie baby
Clinging to its mother's back,
Wanting to keep close.
But when it grows up
The roars are deafening,
Two adult males, fighting for territory.

Have you ever seen a vulture?
They stick together,
Husband and wife, through thick and thin
Cleaning each other's feathers.
But another day, another time, they circle
A death scene, picking the bones
Of rotting animal skeletons.

The beauty of nature
It's so fantastic
The bright flowers bloom
The sparkling ponds ripple.
But when man interferes, nothing's the same
There's fire and destruction
Fighting for territory, they show no mercy.

Imogen Geddes (10)
Aberdour School

Friends

A friend knows you from your head to your toes,
They keep all your secrets that no one else knows,
They're the first to race you to climb a tree,
They pick you up when you've grazed your knee.

A drizzling school morning becomes sunny and bright
As you come through the gates and a friend is in sight,
With news to swap and jokes you can't top,
They can make you laugh until you can't stop.

Arguments happen - but they're soon past.
The day is too short for them to last,
There are games of *'It'* and bikes to ride,
And when it's raining there are cards inside.

A friend will put you back on your feet,
They'll even give you their very last sweet,
A friend sees what is in your heart,
Not how you look or whether you're smart.

Though distance may part you, you know in your heart,
That just as they've always been from the start,
A friend is a person on whom you depend,
Through thick and thin until the end.

Kate Wakefield (9)
Aberdour School

Pets

Megan has two tortoises, two cats; her house is like a zoo,
Matthew has two dogs, a cat; his house is packed tight too.

Francesca has a bulldog; he really likes to play,
Asuka has a lop-eared rabbit; he wants to sleep all day.

Daniel has a hamster; he's shown me a nice drawing,
Guy, my twin, he has no pet, how really, truly boring.

Me, well I have a hamster too, she loves to play in her ball,
Brett has some goldfish, in a tank that's really tall.

Roisin also has some fish, 82, it cannot be denied,
Dominique had a cat, sympathy please, he died.

James has a rat, a fancy rat,
Oliver has two rabbits, big and fat.

Jessica has a kitten and her friendly cat,
Ben, the last but not the least,
He has no pets but he could keep a mini-beast!

Imogen Lester (9)
Aberdour School

My Idol

My idol is a rock star,
And lead singer in a band,
I went to see him at his best,
The best group in the land.

My idol is the coolest,
He can make his guitar sing,
He jumps around on stage a lot,
Of modern rock he *is* the king.

My idol's name is Matt,
Matt Bellamy is his name,
His band is called 'Muse',
And rocking is their game.

Matthew Godden (10)
Aberdour School

My Pet

My furry cuddly pet is feline,
A tabby with a ginger glow,
Above the fish tank she will recline,
On her back her tummy will show.
But if you stroke it do take care,
To check she has no evil glare.

She will not use her brand new bed,
All her special presents are ignored,
Playing with string and conkers instead,
Scratching the sofa opposed to the cord.
She may look cute and soft to the eye,
But inside an evil monster does lie.

She begs for scraps under the table,
She really does adore her food,
To give her extras we are unable,
And when we don't she will brood.
Beware she may be sly and cheat
All for a nice juicy chicken treat.

Antony Kalindjian (11)
Aberdour School

Favourite Things

Riding my bicycle in the park,
Pillow fights with sisters in the dark,
Going shopping for chocolate and sweets,
These are a few of my favourite treats.

PC and TV and PS2,
Can be fun when there's nothing to do,
Playing with friends on a warm summer's day,
Knowing Mum and Dad are not far away.

Sewing and cooking, ballet and gym,
These are as good as having a swim,
Singing and dancing, painting and parties,
These are nearly as good as Smarties!

Holly Sharman (7)
Aberdour School

Seasons

S ome flowers are growing
P retty snowdrops in the sun
R abbits run through the woods
I nsects are coming to life
N ests are full of baby birds
G radually summer is coming.

S easide
U nder the sun
M y brother and me
M ake sandcastles
E very day for a week
R acing in the sea.

A utumn is coming
U nder trees
T umbling leaves on the road
U nder the clear sky
M any bonfires burning
N ow winter is almost here.

W inter is cold and frosty
I ndoors the fire is lit
N ight-time is early
T elevisions are on
E veryone wraps up to walk
R oll on spring.

Oliver Reavley (9)
Aberdour School

Holidays

It's nearly time for my holiday
I don't think I can wait,
It never comes quick enough
That I can state.

When I go on holiday
I like to see the sea
And walking up and down the beach
This always fills me with glee.

Whether the holiday is near water
Or in the middle of town,
I always have a good time
I never have a frown.

Last year I went to Paris
I saw all of the sights
I even ate some French food
And it didn't give me the frights.

This year I'm going to Devon
I'll walk, sail and climb
I know it'll be like Heaven
I'll have a wicked time.

Ralph Haville (9)
Aberdour School

Holidays

Holidays are a time to play,
Sometimes we stay at home,
Sometimes we go away,
But I don't mind what we do.

Portugal was sunny and hot,
We didn't want to do a lot,
We spent long lazy days by the pool,
And no one had to go to school.

Florida was fun in a different way,
To an exciting theme park we went each day,
Epcot, Magic Kingdom to name just two,
There certainly was plenty for us to do.

Scotland is often cold but cheery,
The journey there is long and weary,
The same is true of Wales you know,
But it's not quite so far to go.

Holidays happen throughout the year,
At Christmas, Easter and summer too,
Whatever the weather, let's be clear,
We have fun - how about you?

Guy Lester (9)
Aberdour School

Families

Some families are big,
Some families are small.
Some children have no family,
While others have it all.

My family is big,
My family is mad.
Together we make six,
With 2 girls, 2 boys, Mum and Dad.

My mum is the best,
Even when she shouts.
My dad is brilliant,
Especially when he's about.

So everyone out there,
Please remember,
You will always have someone to love you
When you are part of a family like that!

Eiméar Monaghan (9)
Aberdour School

My Favourite Things Old And New

'The Golf Ball'

In 1590 it was made of wood
And early golfers had to be very good.
By 1790 they were using a 'feathery'
On Scottish links, which are quite 'heathery'.
Gooses down stuffed into leather
Did not fair well in northern weather.

In 1850 came the 'Gutta Percha',
Made of rubber and easy to purchase.
By now the Scots were going golf nutty
And in 1880 came the 'machine gutty'.
The 'haskell' two piece had a core
And fewer golfers shouting 'fore'!

The modern ball has lots of dimples
And Ian Woosnams driving gives me goose pimples.
My favourite is a Titleist four,
Which most pros play on the PGA tour.
What you use is up to you -
Trusty 'old' or lucky 'new'.

David Boote (11)
Aberdour School

My Pet

My dog is called Gemma,
I hope she never dies,
She's honest and true,
And would never tell lies.

I love her so much,
She's the best dog I know,
She's ever so funny,
When she plays in the snow.

She's got a big furry coat,
Which is the colour of honey,
She's got big dark eyes,
And her nose is always runny.

She's cute and cuddly,
On her I can depend,
She's such a good dog,
She's my best friend.

James Barlow (9)
Aberdour School

My Pet Dragon

My pet, he is a dragon,
His eyes are deep, deep red.
His teeth are as sharp as daggers,
His scales are as hard as lead.

During the night he flies out,
Searching for his prey.
But instead of bringing mice back,
He brings kids who've lost their way.

My dragon, he breathes fire,
And sets my stuff alight.
The flame as red as ruby,
And my stuff left black as night.

My dragon may sound scary,
But he wouldn't hurt a fly.
Because he's in my imagination,
And there he shall always lie.

Alex Huber (11)
Aberdour School

Fireworks

(Based on 'Fireworks' by James Reeves)

They rise like flaming arrows
That shoot upon the night,
Then come down to Earth
From a great height.

They unfold like uncurling woodlice
And exploding dynamite
Speeding through the night.

Rockets and Catherine wheels
Make a colourful parade in the sky
Where spinning balloons twist forever.

Henry Charatan & Luc Turnbull (8)
Aldro School

Fireworks

(Based on 'Fireworks' by James Reeves)

They rise like a flaming missile
Heading towards its target,
That explodes in the night sky
Then they drop like dead flies.

They unfold like an umbrella
In a gust of wind,
And a jellyfish
That is about to eat its prey.

Rockets and Catherine wheels
Make a circus of the sky
When they rotate with exploding colours.

Rory Govan (9) & Farai Matanga (8)
Aldro School

Fireworks

(Based on 'Fireworks' by James Reeves)

They rise like furious shooting stars
Fighting for attention
Surely, surely that one's ours
Maybe that one's yours.

They unfold like flower buds
That result in sparkling flames
Blasting up through the air
Coming to a halt.

Rockets and Catherine wheels
Make an artistic mess of the sky.

MacGregor Cox (9) & Richard Gray (8)
Aldro School

Fireworks

(Based on 'Fireworks' by James Reeves)

They rise like a gun that has shot 60 bullets
That flew through the air and cut it like a pitchfork.

They rise like a jellyfish that has been flattened
They go back to shape and then go up.

Each firework unfolds like a cardboard box
With toys in it, and an umbrella
With diamonds flying out of its centre.

Rockets and Catherine wheels
Make a cinema in the sky,
Like a paintball gun shooting rapidly
With bullets exploding full of all the colours of the rainbow.

Alexis Ralli (9)
Aldro School

Fireworks

(Based on 'Fireworks' by James Reeves)

They rise like flying birds
That are aiming for their prey.
They cut through the air
Like a flaming pitchfork
Then burst like a giant Christmas cracker.

They unfold like a picked flower
Starting to bloom with its beautiful colours
With crimson, blue and yellow
Like a rainbow flowing across the sky.

Rockets and Catherine wheels
Make a circus in the sky.

Adam Skantze (9)
Aldro School

Fireworks

(Based on 'Fireworks' by James Reeves)

They rise like flaming arrows
Shooting through the air,
That explodes into the night.

They unfold like flowers
Opening in the sun,
And an umbrella
Unfolding in the night.
Like a jellyfish
Swimming through the ocean.

Rockets and Catherine wheels
Make a group of colours
To light up the night.

Harrison Charles (8)
Aldro School

Waterfall

Mighty waterfall crashing down.
Splashing water,
Freezing cold, roaring echoes.
Chattering swimmers, cold water.
Wrecks of ships.
Foaming splutters, strong rapids.
People looked amazed, fish jumping out
Water flowing away.

Charlie Bayliss (8)
Aldro School

Fireworks

(Based on 'Fireworks' by James Reeves)

They rise like flaming arrows
That explode into the night,
Then fall to Earth
Like dazzling, whirling petals.

They unfold like a delicate flower
Opening its petals.

Rockets and Catherine wheels
Make a battlefield of the sky
When rifles shoot their bullets off
The enemy flee or die.

Jack Bolton (9)
Aldro School

Fireworks

(Based on 'Fireworks' by James Reeves)

They rise like flaming bombs
That explode into the night,
Then fall like coloured pencils catching alight.

They unfold like a suitcase
Spilling out its contents.

Rockets and Catherine wheels
Make a flaming tornado of the sky.

Alexander Chidgey (8)
Aldro School

Fireworks

(Based on 'Fireworks' by James Reeves)

They rise like a flock of birds
That are migrating to Africa.
Then fall like diving eagles
Trying to catch their prey.

They unfold like a parachute
Falling through the air,
Like an umbrella opening in the rain.

Rockets and Catherine wheels
Spin like chariot wheels on fire.

Thomas Gudgeon (8)
Aldro School

Tornado

Swizzling, swirling,
Fast and strong.
Tornadoes are swirling.
Sounds of *roaring!*
Makes people shudder.

Charlie McKeown (7)
Aldro School

Fireworks

(Based on 'Fireworks' by James Reeves)

They rise like a person who had a gun
Shooting through the air,
That means the star is racing onto the pitch.

Like a star spinning around the race track
With coach Mr Moon wobbling on the pitch.

They unfold like a Christmas cracker
Throwing out Christmas presents,
And an octopus unfolding in the night.

Rockets and Catherine wheels
Make a rainbow in the sky.

Scott Kim (9)
Aldro School

War

Bang! goes the canon from the castle wall.
Boom! goes the machine gun, killing old and small.

Zoom! goes the jet plane, giving me a fright.
Whizz! goes the 'copter, soaring through the night.

'Aarrgh!' say the people, the plane has hit the town.
The army shall surrender, the country's going down!

Adam Bagley (8)
Aldro School

The Magic Box

(Based on 'Magic Box' by Kit Wright)

In my magic box there is . . .
The 13th month when it always snows,
A silver car with light blue stars on it that can take you anywhere,
A rabbit that purrs and lives with a witch.

In my magic box there is . . .
A cat that bounces and loves to eat carrots,
Four gold beans, you plant them and they grow into a beanstalk,
One of Santa's sleigh bells that ring.

In my magic box there is . . .
A Catherine wheel that never stops spinning,
Three pink fairies that cannot fly,
A starfish on an orange beach.

My magic box is . . .
Scarlet-red with cherry diamonds and silver stars on it,
The lid is made of sparkling seashells,
It smells of my mum's perfume.

Laura Egan (8)
Beacon Hill Primary School

A Soldier From World War II

I could see tanks on fire,
Bombs blowing up houses as the sky turned black,
I was walking along when gunshots were heard in the distance.

I could hear bullets fired at the mountain,
My friend's boots splashing in the mud when we went into battle.

I could feel sweat running down my neck as we marched into battle
And my gun rubbed against my leg.

Elliott Baldwin (8)
Beacon Hill Primary School

Behind My Secret Trapdoor

(Inspired by 'Magic Box' by Kit Wright)

Behind my trapdoor there is . . .

An old croaking radio that hasn't been turned off,
A speck of fairy dust and an old wand,
Six smelly socks sleeping in shiny shoes.

Behind my trapdoor there is . . .

A magic hairbrush that brushes your hair on its own,
A hairdryer that sucks you into its fan,
Magic marshmallows, when you eat them you disappear.

Behind my trapdoor there is . . .

A potion, that when you drink it you grow Dracula fangs,
When you drink this toadstool juice you get chickenpox,
Plant these and a grape vine will grow up the side of your house.

Behind my secret trapdoor there is . . .

An old granny holding a bottle of poisoned beer,
Press a button and this chair walks wherever you want,
Maggots munching mouldy marmalade on an ancient crumbling plate

The door of my trapdoor is made of two pieces of glass with water
From the Indian Ocean trapped inside them.
The glass is held up by a frame of twinkling stars fixed together
With moon dust.
Its hinges are made of crab arms.

Siobhan Collman (8)
Beacon Hill Primary School

The Victorian Chimney Sweep

What can you see?

Black dust shivering around me.
I can see hot ash,
I can see black soot surrounding me.

What can you hear?

Wind shivering around me.
Birds singing around me.
I can hear kids screaming in the chimney.

What can you feel?

I can feel my knees bursting out with blood,
I can feel the soot on the walls,
I can feel my sore hands.

What can you smell?

I can smell fire,
I can smell the ash,
I can smell the dust in my nose.

What can you touch?

I can touch the black walls,
I can touch the smelly smoke,
I can touch the dirty soot.

Hollie Lacey (9)
Beacon Hill Primary School

The Magic Box

(Based on 'Magic Box' by Kit Wright)

In my magic box I have . . .
A wise grandpa with an enormous beard with wisdom,
A shape-shifting scientist with grey hair and glasses,
A porky, prickly pig with attitude.

In my magic box I have . . .
A giant spider with wings and a tail,
A burger with a mouth, nose and eyes,
A playful pixie, dazzling with love.

In my magic box I have . . .
A scruffy, ugly mouse with an extra tail,
A never-ending steak, juicy, sweet and scrumptious,
A transforming fish who can live outside water.

My magic box is . . .
Gold, it shines like Heaven,
It has a lock made from titanium, which only opens
at the sound of my voice,
It becomes invisible if anyone else tries to open it.

Jack Cooper (8)
Beacon Hill Primary School

Greek General

I see . . .
My enemy at the bottom of the hill, challenging my forces to a battle,
Arrows bouncing off my men's shields,

I hear . . .
Cries of my enemy's men, and mine,
The endless whoosh of my enemy's arrows and birds flying away
Each time one of my rocks is fired from my catapults.

I feel . . .
The smash of swords against my armour
The shiver of my hands as I fight for my life,
And my warhorse as it jumps up to dodge spears and swords.

Alex Doar (9)
Beacon Hill Primary School

The Magic Box

(Based on 'Magic Box' by Kit Wright)

In my magic box there is . . .
A snowman, which is brown like chocolate.
A lake, which is red like a terrible fire
A horse, which is like the deep blue sea.

In my magic box there is . . .
A magic pencil, which never gets blunt
A magic bottle, which contains my favourite drink
A magic clock, which does not need power to work.

In my magic box there is . . .
A magic pen, which never runs out of ink
A magic writing book, which never runs out of pages
A magic light, which is so bright all the time.

My magic box has a blue ribbon
With horse on top and puppies on both sides
And a pink violet on the box.

Emma Pocock (9)
Beacon Hill Primary School

Defeated

I see . . .
My friend dying beside me,
My city burning to the ground,
My men slaying my foe through the heart.

I hear . . .
My son and wife screaming for their lives,
As the enemy destroyed them,
Hoarse cries in the wind.

I feel . . .
My skin crawls as I hear my wife is dead,
An enemy will die,
A breezy wind, as I was the last one alive.

Jade O'Brien (9)
Beacon Hill Primary School

In My Teacher's Cupboard . . .

(Based on 'Magic Box' by Kit Wright)

In my teacher's cupboard . . .
There was a green slimy cage to lock children in.
A slimy toilet brush to tickle smelly toes.
A red anaconda to put on a child when they're naughty.

In my teacher's cupboard . . .
There was a homework tree to take home for extra homework,
A thick drain with nails sticking out to chuck children in.
Gooey cameras for when children are naughty they spit goo.

In my teacher's cupboard . . .
There was a vicious robot to smack children's smelly bums.
A navy Dementor to suck naughtiness out.
An emerald balloon with spiders in it to scare us.

In my teacher's cupboard . . .
There is a child catcher to lock children in when they're annoying.
A gooey trapdoor that has a hand that grabs children
                                        when they're naughty.
A homework copier to copy extra homework.

The teacher's cupboard was . . .
Covered in green, slimy, horrible goo
With bits of disgusting, foul flies
And an enormous, gold, horrible moth's wing.

The teacher's cupboard was . . .
Guarded by a pack of wolves with vicious teeth and sharp claws
With magic in the corners
And gooey eyeballs on top of the cupboard.

Sam Jefferies (9)
Beacon Hill Primary School

The Trapdoor Under The Cupboard

(Inspired by 'Magic Box' by Kit Wright)

I found under the trapdoor . . .
A corner of a star that is a glowing torch,
A fluffy kitten that barks and bites bones,
A muddy dog that miaows and chases its tail.

I found under the trapdoor . . .
Two smelly socks that Santa fills with mouse droppings,
A horse's tail that Cinderella uses for a brush,
A twinkle of a fairy's wand, which cures all your problems.

I found under the trapdoor . . .
A pig's ear that is a cup for Shrek,
A bit of dinosaur's skin which looks like a coat,
A tie of a zombie, which glows out a signal.

I found under the trapdoor . . .
A postcard, which shows you the world like a TV,
A robot that magics food fit for a king,
Polluted water that poisons you if you are thirsty.

The trapdoor has . . .
A piece of gold going round the handle and fossils to hold it down,
It looked as if the trapdoor is mud, but I knew it was rotted wood,
Even the hinges were all rotting like crumbling bread.

Every single day I will go in
But when I am gone and dead I'll be buried there
So that I can still go and haunt my old house.

Emily Pringle (8)
Beacon Hill Primary School

In My Teacher's Cupboard

(Inspired by 'Magic Box' by Kit Wright)

In my teacher's cupboard . . .
A pen that marks work while the teacher is eating biscuits,
Paper that when you write on will correct your spelling,
Scissors that cut anything into thousands of pieces
                                    and different shapes.

In my teacher's cupboard . . .
A cup of coffee that forces her to give us sweets,
A magic pen that when she writes maths on the whiteboard
It changes to give children playtime,
When the teacher sits down the chair magically moves away.

In the teacher's cupboard . . .
Special glasses so when she's not looking at us
                                    she can see us behind her.
Worksheet with everlasting questions so we don't ever finish.
She waves her wand and forces us to sit down quietly
A magic clock to make sure that when the teacher
Comes into school we're there ready and the classroom is tidy.

Vicky Mehta (8)
Beacon Hill Primary School

The Magic Box

(Based on 'Magic Box' by Kit Wright)

In my magic box there is . . .
A horse that turns into a unicorn before your eyes,
A donkey with glittering hooves that makes him fly,
A fluffy black cat that bounces around and has long ears.

In my magic box there is . . .
A furry rabbit that hunts for mice with tails,
A flower that grows in winter and dies in spring,
A talking tree that tells you jokes.

In my magic box there is . . .
A ship that can go on land and not on sea,
A dragon that breathes water instead of fire,
A net that catches dreams.

My magic box . . .
Looks like a silver violet with horses on it,
When you open it, it plays a song
And it feels like rough glitter.

Megan Witherington (9)
Beacon Hill Primary School

A Roman Soldier

I see . . .
The evil enemy stabbing my friend in his heart,
And our soldiers falling to the ground every second,
My enemies waving their spears and swords each time
                                                  they kill a man.

I hear . . .
My men dying and men shouting victory from the other team,
And the birds trying to get away.

I feel . . .
My sword with blood on it,
And the scars and cuts on my knees and shoulders,
My bow and arrows on my back, which is jabbing into me.

I smell . . .
The blood spilling from the bodies,
The smoke from the fires in my village,
And the sweat from everywhere.

I touch . . .
My sword trying to pull it out,
My heavy armour pulling me down,
And my bow and arrows, which I am firing right now.

Luke Lorimer (9)
Beacon Hill Primary School

In The Darkness

I can see . . .
A bright light flashing above me,
Black soot falling down into my eyes,
Swollen cuts on my hands full of dirt and pus.

I can hear . . .
The crackling fire underneath me,
The master yelling at me telling me to hurry up,
The baker's boy ringing his bell while riding through
                                                    the market outside.

I can feel . . .
My cuts stinging,
The smoke from the fire rushing past me,
The cold and rough walls on the palm of my hand.

Mercedes Lock (9)
Beacon Hill Primary School

The Roman Gladiator

I can see . . .
A sword stabbed through my friend's heart and I hate it.

I can hear . . .
A thump that was a giant rock that crashed to the floor.

I can feel . . .
An earthquake moving along the ground.

I can smell . . .
Fire burning from the city everywhere and blood which smells horrible.

Oliver Wilkinson (9)
Beacon Hill Primary School

In My Teacher's Cupboard

(Inspired by 'Magic Box' by Kit Wright)

In my teacher's cupboard . . .

A broken confiscated cobwebby superman toy with dust over it,
A yellow dusty laptop with grubby pictures of my teacher
in a shabby gown,
The handwriting books that are disgraceful because they
smell of really bad cheese.

In my teacher's cupboard . . .

An apple that is very rotten and it has a really long worm in it,
An old fingered book that has not been opened for a long, long time,
A really scary trapdoor filled with cages for bad children.

In my teacher's cupboard . . .

A skull headed wand to make the children become very smart,
A dusty spell book to make a very bad poison,
Extra watery brains to put in children's heads when they
are very bad.

In my teacher's cupboard . . .

Three spiders to make children tell the truth,
A ruler to whip bad children's bottoms,
Different sweets to knock out people for three hours.

The cupboard has rotten posters of bad witches and
yucky hung mirrors,
I will slide down the narrow trapdoor and free the children
with the keys,
But I might get trapped myself.

Sarah Mayson (9)
Beacon Hill Primary School

In My Wardrobe

(Inspired by 'Magic Box' by Kit Wright)

In my wardrobe there are . . .
Super smelly socks, which make you faint if you smell them,
A monstrous mirror, once you look into it you look like a monster,
A poisoning potion with a flavour of poopy pigs.

In my wardrobe there is . . .
Strangling Shrek, which will make you quiver,
Roman armour, which is *excellent* for fighting,
10,000 Cadburys chocolate bars, best in the world.

In my wardrobe is a . . .
Headless chicken that will chop off your head,
Walking shoes which walk when no one's feet are in them,
An invisibility cloak, once you put it on you are invisible.

In my wardrobe are some . . .
Super shoes with super bounce action,
A super car with amazing auto drive,
An amazing camera, which can take three pictures at once.

My wardrobe looks like an ice world,
It smells like a pigsty,
With icicles hanging from the ceiling.

Tom Newman (8)
Beacon Hill Primary School

Yellow Shoes

Yellow shoes are the best
They are better than the rest.
Yellow is the colour of custard
Yellow is the colour of mustard.
Yellow shoes on my feet
They make me look really neat.
Yellow is the colour of custard
Yellow is the colour of mustard.
Yellow shoes with yellow bows
Neatly wrapped around my toes.
Yellow is the colour of custard
Yellow is the colour of mustard.
Yellow shoes look so fine
Make me get to school on time.
Yellow is the colour of custard
Yellow is the colour of mustard.
Walking high walking low
Yellow shoes wherever I go.
Yellow is the colour of custard
Yellow is the colour of mustard.

Gabrielle Thomas (8)
Cranmer Primary School

Sports

Let's play tennis
Not with menace.
Let's have a swimming race
Try and keep up the pace.
The last one is football
Let's play in the hall.
Sport is great
Sport is fun
It is good for everyone!

Ammar Haque (7)
Cranmer Primary School

Art

It's art today,
Hip hip hooray,
We're using paint and paper,
We have plenty left for later.

It's art today,
Hip hip hooray,
People using brushes,
Blinking their eyelashes.

It's art today,
Hip hip hooray,
Let's make a pot,
It's going to be so hot!

It's art today,
Hip hip hooray,
Let's draw a hawk,
With our coloured chalk.

Emily Potter (8)
Cranmer Primary School

Computers

A computer is a special thing.
It can even help you sing.
A computer uses a special mouse
Not the pet you have in a house.
A computer lets you write
And I can build a website.
I always search the net
I did not do anything yet.
You need a screen
Otherwise it will be mean
A computer has a tower
Which gives it power.

Ryan Rae-Daniel (7)
Cranmer Primary School

Colours

Red is the colour of a healing heart
Yellow is the colour of the sun, which never breaks apart
Blue is the colour of the beautiful sky
White is the colour that reaches so high.
Green is the colour of a swaying tree
Pink is the one colour that's nice to me
Purple is the colour of joy and faith.
Orange is the colour that makes you feel safe
Gold is the colour that shines so bright
Silver is the colour that sparkles at night
Black is the colour of the night.
Brown is the colour of an owl in flight.

Chloe Chapman (7)
Cranmer Primary School

West Ham

I'm a very big fan of West Ham,
I like them more than bread and jam
I watch them with my old man,
He drinks his beer,
While I sing and cheer,
I wave my scarf
We have a good laugh,
Their colours are really cool.
They're better than school,
West Ham, West Ham, West Ham.

Reece Owen-White (7)
Cranmer Primary School

My Garden Pond

Big and round that's my garden pond.
In the deep dark water, live exciting things.
The fish splash around making waves,
Splish-splash, splish-splash.
They swim between the wavy plants waiting for dinner time.
I throw the food and watch the fish pushing and shoving.
The frog sees the food, *hop, splash.*
He swims across the pond to get the food.
He swims to the other side and hops off,
The pond will still be there tomorrow,
But I don't know about the fish, I have got a big cat!

Kelly Wilson (7)
Cranmer Primary School

Olympics

Running and jumping, swimming in the pool
Get those arms pumping don't want to look a fool.
Racing round the track running as fast as you can
Getting past the pack a gold medal's the plan.
Gymnastics on the mat
Cartwheels are great
Go easy on those weights.
The marathon has started
Watch out for the wall
Enjoy the Olympics
The greatest event of all.

John McCoy (8)
Cranmer Primary School

Medieval Times

(Inspired by the medieval game 'Runescape')

Everybody kills each other
Come on people do it for your mother.
Oh look, an axe
I'm going to say hello to Max.

Oh my God, a shield!
Uh oh, it's in a cornfield,
This man has two swords
Oh look, it's the lords.

Someone is going to trade me a pickaxe
I'm going to trade them nick nacks.
I need a double-sided battleaxe
Bubble to glide; here's funny Max.

My God I need some armour
Look! There's a level seven farmer,
Do you see a pair of boots?
I can make wooden flutes.

Here's a rat, level three
Watch out people it's killing me,
What do you have in your bank?
Is your name Frank?

I have to go, Mum's calling me
Ready to lay the table for tea.

Andrew Lyndon (8)
Cranmer Primary School

Pets

Pesky pets are what I like
They may give you a terrible fright,
Spiders really frighten my mother
No pet on Earth could frighten my brother.
Guinea pigs and hamsters too
You should really love them too.

Milo Mitchell (7)
Cranmer Primary School

My Cat

My cat is the one I love in my family
I love my cat and he loves me
My cat is very fat
I love my cat
My mum and dad love him as well.
My cat plays with me
We jump up and down together.
My cat is nice and kind too.
I love my cat
In the summer my cat catches butterflies with me
He tries to stalk birds in the summer
He is very cheeky but very nice too.
I love him and he loves me.

Sarah Mepham (7)
Cranmer Primary School

About The Summer Sun

The sun is hot and bright.
Splashing in my pool and drying in the sun,
What great fun
A tan is what I get when playing in the sun.
Playing water fights with my friends.
I'll get them back with the hose.
What are those?
Freckles on my nose,
The days are long in the summer
The summer is out all day.
That's good for me, more time to play.

Robyn Milton (7)
Cranmer Primary School

The Ocean Sea

The ocean sea is a dangerous place to be
Sharks shiver and hunt their tea.
Where dolphins just keep out of the sea,
Fish swim happily and cheerfully
Jellyfish wobble and juggle around.
Stingrays lay on the sandy ground.
Sharks swim in the deep blue sea
And keep their eyes peeled for their tea
Penguins slide around the icy shore.
In the olden days they sailed with big sails and oars.

Paige Smith (7)
Cranmer Primary School

Winter

Windy, windy wonderland,
Ivy's climbing on the frosty ground,
Night-time stars twinkling bright
A clear black sky, what a sight
Tea and biscuits for the old man,
Eating chocolate 'til you're sick and brown
So now the day has ended, let it be a peaceful night,
And wish you a happy dream, without the winter cold sight . . .

Anisa Khatun (8)
Cranmer Primary School

My Goldfish

My goldfish never bothers me
But the only thing that bothers her is fleas
My goldfish is so clever,
She's never wrong, ever.
When she blows a bubble
She never gets in trouble.
My goldfish is the perfect pet
She never gets sick to go to the vet.

Clement Olutola (8)
Cranmer Primary School

Tsunami Poem

It makes me sad because people have died,
All of the wild sea covered their homes,
And children were crying
People climbed trees for safety
But even the trees fell in the flood.
It makes me feel how lucky I am to be living in England
Away from the danger.

Liam Hill (8)
Cranmer Primary School

Lovely Food

I like eating lots of food
It puts me in a really good mood.
Most of all, I like chips
It makes me want to lick my lips.
Burgers I love to eat
Especially ones with lots of meat.

Romelo Sinclair (8)
Cranmer Primary School

Toys

Toys are toys,
Some made for girls,
Some made for boys.
Girls put curls in every strand of hair
Whilst boys are sitting on wooden chairs
My friend Skye has a playroom
And I just have the room of doom,
It's always a mess
When I am trying to find my dress.

The moles are stealing my Barbie dolls
And I'm only eight years old.
My toys are never easy to find
When the church bell has only just chimed.
I have a brown bear
He is on my shelf
I've also got a tiny green elf
There are lots of things on my shelf
But most of all I like myself.

Leah Green (8)
Cranmer Primary School

I'm The Wind

I'm the wind,
No one can see me!
I'm the wind,
But people can feel me!
I'm the wind,
No one can help me!
I'm the wind,
The trees sway with me!

Natalie Ashen (8)
Cranmer Primary School

Fishing

There are many different kinds of fish
You can eat some fish on a dish
Different fish in the deep blue sea
You can have a cup of tea.
Some fish dip and dive all day
They often dive in the month of May
Carp have bright slimy scales
Sometimes when I catch a fish I turn pale.

Thomas Owen (8)
Cranmer Primary School

My Family

My mum just had a baby, my dad is helping out.
My new baby sister's bawling
Because she wants her milk from her bottle, but it won't release.

My big sister Yadah is walking home from school with Kaprice
My sister Kaalei is playing with her friend Britney
But whenever I go in her playground they always chase me.

Okubea Thompson (8)
Cranmer Primary School

The Stupid Football Poem

The ball is like a big tomato,
The goals are like a bridge,
The nets are like big waffles
And don't forget the pitch.

Now if you get a chance to go there,
You better beware
Because the players are big
But the ref is small.

Of course I'm being stupid
But that's what I do best,
So if you get a chance to go there,
Don't forget your vest.

Now the ball is like a tomato,
The goal is like a bridge,
The nets are like big waffles
And don't forget the pitch.

Adam Baker (11)
Furzefield Primary School

Butterflies

B utterflies flitter,
U nder glitter,
T hey sparkle and shine,
T hey love this rhyme,
E verlasting friend,
R eally, they twist and bend,
F orever yours,
L ike opening doors,
I f ever forgotten,
E ver always rotten,
S o never forget this poem.

Laura Jones (10)
Furzefield Primary School

The Storm

The storm banging on the window sill,
The whole world quiet and still.
It feels like all the world has frost
And the wind is howling like a ghost.

The storm is blowing down the trees,
With a really, really chilly breeze.
There are no people in my sight,
This is giving me a fright.

'The storm is all around the world,'
I think that's what I have heard.
At last the storm goes away
And everyone goes, 'Hooray!'

It might come back again
And try and give us lots of pain.
Please be really aware
And as always please take care.

Joel Babu (10)
Furzefield Primary School

The Terrible School

School is the worst place to be, believe me Mum, I plea.
It feels like a prison, you can't stop going until sixteen.
It looks as boring as going to sleep.
The dinners look like slop, as for the water fountain -
It always likes to stop.
You'll surely want to be me, not!

Jazmine Parker (10)
Furzefield Primary School

My Body

I've got music in my footy,
I've got singing in my eary,
But when I shout
My head starts to shake about.

There is wiggling in my botty,
There are animal sounds coming out of my mouth.
My armpits start to smell,
But when I laugh, my fingers start to swell.

My body is like a rocket when I'm running,
On sports day I always come 1st place.
But most of the time,
The boys are playing kiss chase.

Now I hope you liked my poem,
It's not hard to see,
That this poem has butterflies
In my hairies.

Hannah Glasgow (10)
Furzefield Primary School

The Crying Storm

Drawing closer and closer to the edge.
The storm is crying, the thunder is wailing.
Shooting lightning bolts through the sky.
Sniggering like an African jo-jo bird,
It has a certain rhythm to wake,
But this is why it is the crying storm
And as we sleep, safe and snug,
It howls like a wolf in its forest.

Farida Pashi (10)
Furzefield Primary School

My Friend, Sophie

My friend, Sophie,
Well, what can I say?
Sometimes she can be very quiet,
But can also make a loud riot.

Sophie is super fab
And she doesn't drool,
But she doesn't drive a mini cab,
She is really cool.

Sophie is really, really cool
And she never looks nerdy.
She's really funny
And always wears Burberry.

So now you've heard of my best friend, Sophie,
Go home and pretend you're topsy-turvy.

Stephanie Cole (11)
Furzefield Primary School

My Dog, Sam

My dog, Sam
Likes to eat ham.
My dog, Sam
Looks like a lamb.
My dog, Sam
Watching Bam Bam
Whilst he's wearing his jim-jams.
He wakes me up in the morning,
Whilst I'm still snoring,
Oh my dog,
Sam!

Lewis O'Callaghan (11)
Furzefield Primary School

The Planets

The planets, Mercury, Venus, Mars and more,
Float in space like huge balloons
And have many, many moons.
Some are red, some are blue,
Some are multicoloured too!
Some have rings that look like floats,
Others are as small as boats.

Some are giant balls of gas,
Others are just a lump of mass.
Others have some living things,
But no bigger than most pins.

So as you see,
Some planets can be,
Very interesting things.
Some are light, some are dark,
Others only house a spark.
So as you see,
Some planets can be,
Very interesting things.

Shaun Bowie (11)
Furzefield Primary School

The Diary

It's someone's diary, heh, heh, heh,
It's secret, it's red and it's . . . empty, *oh!*
It's a human with no insides
And it's red paint.
I feel annoyed that it's empty,
As annoyed as my brother when my dog annoys him,
The diary makes me think of total emptiness.

Tommy Bauldry (11)
Furzefield Primary School

American Theme Parks

Roller coasters as fast as a cheetah hunting deer,
Merry-go-rounds as slow as a tortoise,
Attractions as fun as the corner shop,
Candyfloss as tasty as a roast lamb.

The slides as colourful as a pattern,
The Ferris wheel as boring as history,
The River Rapids as cold as the Antarctic,
The Freefall as high as a plane.

And, *cor blimey,* was that Freefall high,
But it is great,
Islands of Adventures, *cor, that's fun too,*
It's in America, in Florida.

Roller coasters are great,
Especially in Busch Gardens,
Lots of coasters, fast ones too,
But I'm glad I went, you should try it today.

Busch Gardens is as big as an airport, maybe bigger.
Islands of Adventures - as fun as can be.
Disney, more colourful than a multicoloured coat.
I'm glad I went, I am, I am, I am.

Ben Grogan (10)
Furzefield Primary School

My Friend

A friend never leaves you when you're down,
Kind, sweet and beautiful like a kitten,
Who is as soft as a rug,
They make me feel happy,
A friend makes me think of relaxation.

Lejla Palmer (11)
Furzefield Primary School

My Thumb

My thumb was very big and it looked like a twig,
It sat on my hand every day, singing *hip hip hooray!*
I would look at the sun like a hot bun
And fiddle with my thumb.

Until the time had come to say goodnight,
The next morning my thumb woke up like a red-hot bun.
It woke me up by twitching me
And I shouted, 'Hey!
Why did you do that?'
'Because you're late for school.'
My thumb comes with me,
It gets me into trouble by flicking paper sometimes.

So now you know what my thumb's like,
So don't let your thumb become like mine.

Daniel Giannetta (9)
Furzefield Primary School

The Trash

The trash pile was quite high
And no one would take it out,
It was a skunk's nest,
It had swelled to amount.
Kaboom! the truck was a wreck.
Worse than soup that's sucked,
As big as Everest, it rotted up
And became Mount Stinky,
As stinky as a skunk's nest
And as high as the sky,
Mount Stinky vanished in the night,
Along with every fly.

Ryan Oldridge (10)
Furzefield Primary School

Jabber-Oakley

(Based on 'Jabberwocky' by Lewis Carroll)

'Twas Wednesday night and the slimy kids
Did grumble and groan in the doorway.
Most of the kids look like squids
And so did the exchange from Norway.

Beware of the bouncy castle, my friend,
The people who squash and squish,
Or you'll be bounced to Lands End
And end up like a fish.

She took her DJ earmuffs
And blasted out a deadly sound.
Kids ran from the Oakley for the awful guff,
It hurt like a ground pound.

Rachael Scarsbrook (10)
Furzefield Primary School

Bed!

Deep, deep down, down,
Into the darkness I go.
It is as snug,
As a bug in a rug
And it's the colour of indigo.

This thing that I am describing to you,
Is as thick as the side of my head.
It's made out of wood,
As I knew that it should,
This wonderful thing is a bed!

Andrew Salmon (11)
Furzefield Primary School

Mr Blabber Bocky

(Based on 'Jabberwocky' by Lewis Carroll)

'Twas boring and his slimy nose,
Did tire and linger when he spoke.
All glittery were his shiny clothes,
His hair, *oh boy, was that a joke!*

Beware Mr Blabber Bocky,
The jaws that open, the words that bore.
If you don't listen, he'll give you a shock,
You'll get a kiss and you're on the floor.

He took his vorpal post-it notes,
Long time till he read them,
The students ran just for their coats
And never saw him again.

And as in frightening shock, he stood,
Mr Blabber Bocky with eyes of flame
Rushed to the door and saw he could,
Never work there again!

One, two! One, two! And through! And through!
The vorpal notes went forth and back.
Two, one! Two, one!
Realised he was dumb
And went galumphing in sorrow back!

'And who has sacked Mr Blabber Bocky?
Come to my office my clever boys.
Oh fantastic day, callooh callay,'
They chortled in their joy.

'Twas boring and his slimy nose
Did tire and linger when he spoke,
All glittery were his shiny clothes,
His hair, *oh boy, was that a joke!*

Karina Saul (10)
Furzefield Primary School

Teachers

Teachers can be cool,
Most of the time they're not.
They're as thick as doormats,
None of them are hot.

Their clothes are goofy like nerds',
They have no sense of fashion,
Where the girls have,
We have a fashion passion.

The Year 5/6 teachers,
What can I say?
Don't you feel sorry for us?
We have to see them every day.

English, maths and science,
They are really boring,
As boring as a cardboard box,
Most of the time we're snoring.

Teachers, teachers,
As boring as can be,
That's my poem on teachers,
You would hate to be me.

Hannah Banks (10)
Furzefield Primary School

Robots

Robots as funny as two legs,
Robots as hard as wood,
Robots as stiff as spoons,
Robots clingy as prunes.

They talk all on one note,
They walk like they've got a piece of wood between their legs,
They blink like they haven't got any oil there,
They sing like . . . that's just the thing,
They can't!

Jasmin Saul (9)
Furzefield Primary School

My Cat, Sassy

My cat, Sassy,
Oh, what a lump.
Sometimes she's annoying,
I want to give her a thump.

My cat, Sassy,
She's so sweet,
When she's good,
I'll give her a treat.

My cat, Sassy,
She's so lazy.
She's very fat,
She's got a sister called Daisy.

My cat, Sassy,
She eats a lot.
She's very fat,
Sometimes I think she'll pop.

My cat, Sassy,
She's now gone to sleep.
So be very quiet
And don't make a peep.

Sophie O'Neill (10)
Furzefield Primary School

The Disaster

The disaster is not like us,
But it is very annoying when it occurs,
Exactly like my sister.
Annoying, chaos and boring,
Identical to my brother,
It is an angry giant, I'd say like my dad.
It is a fireball, very like my mum,
As hot as fire, like my dad's dog.
The disaster, very annoying like
A nuclear explosion.

Seamus Brannagan (9)
Furzefield Primary School

Teachers

Teachers think they're smart,
But they're not very good at art.
They dress in suits,
Which makes them look like a bunch of roots.

Teachers, what are they good at?
They're as fat as a cat.
Lazy, but naughty,
They're not even good at that.

As skinny as a plank
Or as fat as a tank.
As mean as a lion,
They can't even use the iron.

Now I don't have to tell you the rest,
Did you know they even wear a vest?
Now, I don't mean to be horrible,
But the teachers are terrible.

Mukaoso Agwuegbo (10)
Furzefield Primary School

The Oracle

The oracle -
It knows all that there is to know.
It is a god shining with light
And the body thought of by a great mind.
Lighter in weight than a feather.
Any question that is asked shall be answered.
The mind of an angel is nothing compared to the oracle.
It makes me feel like a small being.
The oracle is a fulfilled prophecy,
Makes me think of . . .

Ben Murphy (11)
Furzefield Primary School

Space

The universe is a big place; cold, hot and dark.
The hundreds of galaxies, stars and planets
And asteroids drifting around the universe,
Like they won't stop.
Massive stars shine like dots of light
In a pitch-black sky,
Comets flash by as streaks of light.
Planets, blue, green and white,
Red and grey,
The solar systems of the universe
Are as strange as they look.

Peter Rook (11)
Furzefield Primary School

Freaked Out!

Should I go in? I asked myself,
Looking at the deserted house.
I could see paint peeling
And shadows appearing.
The grass was hiding my feet,
I could stand it no longer,
I turned and ran.
I'll come back at dawn tomorrow, I thought,
I'll come back at dawn tomorrow.

So I got my stuff
And went there once again.
I noticed a new white tablecloth
And then I saw the door knocker,
Knocking, knocking, knocking.
I saw the door knocker knocking.
For I never noticed the big red eyes
Watching me all the time
And when I entered, the door went *slam!*
I've never escaped.

Lauren Godin (9)
Grand Avenue Primary School

The Creepy House

The creepy house is surrounded with branches and trees,
I can hear the roaring wind, blowing at my whole body and everywhere.
The spiky grass prickling my legs,
I can hear creepy voices around me.

I step into the house and smell old, mouldy food,
The worst smell was the mouldy cheese.
I entered the house . . .
Objects, cobwebs sticking everywhere, especially on the wall.
All sorts of animals are around the house.
I can hear footsteps getting faster and faster.
I hear a scream.
I run as fast as I can.
Who is it?
What is it
Or am I just dreaming?

Amir Patel (9)
Grand Avenue Primary School

Knocking, Knocking

'Can you pay attention and open the door?'
I yelled loudly and impatiently.
I could see an old, cracked window and a shimmering light.
It was as bright as a brand new penny.
I felt worried and scared, there were butterflies in my stomach.
'Is there anybody there?' I called again,
Staring at the cracks on the walls.
I could hear an echoing of my voice rising to the empty sky.
I felt the roaring wind crawling up my thigh.
I knocked. I knocked again, but harder, feeling the solid centre.
I felt a drop of cold water running down my chest.
I felt bumpy goosebumps around my covered body.
Then I saw a funny-shaped hole in the door.

Emma Mills (10)
Grand Avenue Primary School

The Mystery In The Building

'I've come to collect you,' said the childminder,
Walking on the mystery building's floor,
There were hundreds of voices coming from in the building,
After the childminder came in, he closed the door.

Suddenly, there was an eerie silence,
There was pitch-black as all the lights went out,
Someone was round the corner as a light started to appear,
There was not even a mouse whisker about.
He ran outside to find a different entrance,
To his surprise, in a window was a light.
There were skulls under his feet,
He climbed the building, it took all of his might.

It took him 30 minutes to reach the room,
And at last he found the kids.
They were sitting down
And they were playing a game with lids.

He got them out the window,
Behind them was a ghost
And it made them scream,
They ran to and started the car,
Everyone wished it was a dream.

Owen Cain (10)
Grand Avenue Primary School

Spook

'Twas midnight and I was lost,
As I stared upon the frost.
I needed somewhere to stay,
I could not be there day by day.

And I reached upon a tower,
I had needed some more power.
'Are you there, anyone please?' I said.
All I heard was the banging in my head.

As I heard the owls hooting,
As I heard the hunters shooting.
Then I saw their dusty faces,
I couldn't keep up with their paces.
They were all shouting for me,
For all that I could see.
They needed my help,
But all I could do was yelp.

They were banging on the doors,
They were stamping on the floors.
This wasn't it,
Not one bit.

So I got on my horse,
With all my force
And . . .
Disappeared.

Roxanne Mehdizadeh (9)
Grand Avenue Primary School

The Traveller's Wife

'Please, my wife is ill,' cried the traveller,
Sinking to his knees at the gate.
Nothing could bring him comfort now,
But to know his wife would not be sealed in fate
And at the door of the church ran a squeaking mouse,
So the clock warned him from above.
He repeated his wish, loud and clear again,
For someone to save his love
And yet, in the highest window,
The lamp of hope still glows
And out of the door runs an old man
That the hopeful traveller knows.

They sit at the candlelit table to eat,
Then lay in a bed to rest.
The man gives the medicine to the traveller,
Then rides to his wife for the best.
He reached his wife the next day morn,
Great medicine he gave.
He went back to the kindly man,
His wife, this man did save.

Joy Nunn (10)
Grand Avenue Primary School

The Ghost Of Nobody

'I'll just go, shall I?' stammered the traveller,
Knocking on the rusty old door
And the candles shivered
In the darkening hall.
In the dark, there was an owl hooting,
The sound of a bell
And a tree pulled by the root.
The traveller mounted his horse
And soon the hooves were gone.
The hours crawled by
And the jewel hung high.
A hooded man came out,
A single leaf blew through the man
And to the gates he ran.
Took one look outside
And went back inside.

Zhuohan Li (10)
Grand Avenue Primary School

The Traveller

'Hello, is anyone there?' said the traveller,
Frantically banging on the old rusty door.
But the only response he had,
Was the sound of creaky floors
And the headless phantom danced with laughter
On the dusty, broken boards
And while he was doing that,
His wife did the house chores
And the cats started screeching
And the crows started weeping
And there was a scream from the heights tower,
Which lasted for over an hour.
From that day on, no one knew what had gone wrong,
For the traveller had gone.

Kiran Jabbal (9)
Grand Avenue Primary School

The Zombie Zoo

'Can you tell me where I am?' said the hunter,
Banging on the moonlit door
And the glass window smashed,
As a mouse squeaked whilst running down the hall.
And as it got more into day,
An organ started to play.
'What is going on?'
And no one answered.
Suddenly a light went on.
In a flash the house was gone.
'Oh my God.'
Then zombies came up,
Tugging at the man.
Suddenly he was gone underground.
The zombies strapped him to a table.
'We are going to kill you!'
'No!'
And the hunter was *never* seen again.

Samuel Liles (9)
Grand Avenue Primary School

Midnight House

I walk across the green grabbing grass,
Will I come out alive?
I can feel shivers up my cold and wet feet,
Still thinking *will I survive?*
I carry on through the thick grass,
All shivery and wet, cold and muddy.

Finally, the moment comes
To knock on the creepy door.
All of a sudden, bats come out in my way.
I'm trapped inside - *'Help me!'* I scream.
All shivery and cold in the moonlight.

Samantha West (9)
Grand Avenue Primary School

Will You Ever Come Back?

'Is there anybody there?' said the traveller,
Knocking at the old, creaking door
And as a mysterious man let him in,
His cloak obviously tore.

And a silent old house it was,
But so clean and not a mouse,
There was a shadow, a shadow on the wall.
A skull, a skull on the table it was.

And in the stairway there was a scent of danger
And decay and I had a fear of
If I would be OK.

And there was a moment in the bathroom,
A scary one at that,
A ghost in the smallest mirror,
One with a little black cat.

And the scariest thing was,
A deer's head on a little piece of wood on the wall
And the weird thing was,
The head was in the hall
And the house was on a pier.

Fiona Johnstone (9)
Grand Avenue Primary School

Cottage Chaos

I hear the wind whistling in my face.
I hear an owl hooting in the rustling trees.
I see a glass wobbling in the window.
I hear the door creaking back and forth in the wind.
I hear floorboards creaking under my feet.
I see a full moon in the moonlit sky.
I feel shivers going down my spine.
I see leaves waving in the trees.
It's all there, or is it my imagination?

Peter Clarke (9)
Grand Avenue Primary School

Forest Fern

Up in the ancient, trusty forest,
There upon a tree lived a bird's rusty egg.
Wolves howling in the darkness with all their glee,
Foxes crying with broken hearts
And owls staring at the black cloaked man,
Who ran, and ran, and ran.
Into the middle he sprinted,
While he was sprinting, he could hear,
Trees rustling, something moving, voices echoing,
Leaves crunching,
Squirrels running, hedgehogs rummaging,
Rabbits scampering and a hunter hunting.
'Oh stop reading, somebody's coming.
Quick, hurry, get into this castle.'
The man quickly sprawls along.
'Now it's safe, you can come out and read the rest.'
He could smell the fresh winter's night.
He could feel the sweat of heat.
He could taste the hungriness of his breath.
He could see the thick, thorny bushes
And he could hear the rain rushing down like a waterfall.
Yet he leaves now.
'Is it morning yet?'

Nishalini Ravindran (9)
Grand Avenue Primary School

The Survivor

'Help, can anyone help me?' said the survivor
As he staggered through the forbidden forest.
'Is anybody here or I'm going to die otherwise,' bellowed the survivor
On his way up the hill.
In the distance there was a house,
'I'm going to live!' whispered the survivor
As he came up the hill and heard thousands of voices.
'Show yourself!' shouted the hooded man,
While he soared across the rocky drive.
Knock, knock, knock, the lost man did.
'Is anybody there?' said the frustrated man.
'Can anybody help me?'
Unaware that he was just about to seal his fate
To the phantom listeners inside.
The owner came to the door with no head,
Because he had lost it at war.
'Let me in!' shouted the frightened man.
'Of course,' said the zombie!

Sam Presland (10)
Grand Avenue Primary School

The Listeners

'I am here for it,' screeched the traveller,
Bashing the inn doors.
The hungry horse chewed his coat,
The coat he wore for his wars
And a shadow in the darkness screamed,
The melancholy traveller cried.
The rusty window showed his lover's heart,
He could smell the smell of someone who'd died.
The heartbroken traveller sobbed out his eyes.
'Why did I tell all those lies?'
He bashed the doors, he wanted it so.
He went away and said his goodbyes.
He heard a cry of sadness in the church.
Trot, trot, trot, iron on stone.
'Wait, wait, wait, one last one, wait!'
'Stop, or I will moan.'
His lover's heart runs up to him,
He runs away, 'Why? Why?'
If you run, I will just go.
Fine then, goodbye, goodbye.

Jessica Stanhope (10)
Grand Avenue Primary School

The Thing

'Is anybody there?' the man yelled,
The wind started to blow like horses running free,
The door opened, nobody was there.
'Hello?' the man called again.
He felt chills through his spine.
He took a few steps in,
There was a flickering light flashing through the moonlit light.
The wind blew again, but . . .
Slam!
The door was locked.
Going further and further into the house.
He had to find the key,
But where was it?
Was it here or was it there?
Confusion was all around him,
Five dusty halls he had to choose.
Would he go to the slug room
Or the incredibly deadly bedroom?
There was a shimmer on the floor,
It looked like a key,
He picked it up.
Running and running, closer and closer,
He was free!
You would hear an oven boiling like mad,
Silence once again.

Natalie Leon-Guerrero (10)
Grand Avenue Primary School

The Ultimate Scream

The doors creaked slowly,
Bugs crawled in and out of the doors.
I saw the remains of the trophy room,
I found the door, but it was locked,
I needed to go to the toilet,
But it was all rusty.
The whole house was dusty,
I heard a *drip, drip, drip*.
I went back to the toilet
And the tap was dripping,
I turned it off.
All the lights flickered off.
I ran out of the house,
The grass was long and curly,
The tree looked like it was alive,
The gate to the front garden,
I couldn't get it open,
But the hinges were broken,
So I kicked it, it snapped in half.
I went into the front garden,
I heard a blood-curdling cry,
I ran screaming from the house.

George Bolton (9)
Grand Avenue Primary School

Vampire

It was midnight everywhere, *dong!*
I woke with a fright.
'Phew! Only a dong from Big Ben!'
Ever since we moved here
I've been so scared to hear
The creak of my door, yep, I'm a kid,
Only I . . . I heard . . . yep, I did.

Then it said, 'Ah-ha, I've found it!'
Then suddenly I heard it bite,
I heard a wolf really,
I escaped very, very nearly.
'Heeeelp!' I cried.
But it seemed everyone had died.
But I had turned into . . .

What had bitten me?

Anand Majithia (10)
Grand Avenue Primary School

The Listeners

'Open the door,' bellowed the traveller.
Kicking the old door,
An owl hooted in the trees,
Dust carpeted the floor,
A wolf howled in the distance.
Birds flew overhead,
With wind in the traveller's ears,
Only one man wasn't in bed
And there is a glowing red light.
Suddenly, there was a purple glow,
Cobwebs were hanging everywhere,
There were mysterious footprints in the snow.

Emily Quinn (9)
Grand Avenue Primary School

Escape!

I could feel it, I had to keep running,
Maybe I'll never find my way out.
I strutted across a mossy log,
But I kept on running.
I didn't know where I was going, but I kept running.
I had grazed my knee and it was bleeding.
I could feel the wind whizzing through my skin.
I felt a close presence through the trees.
I looked around, I saw eyes all around me.
I had a sudden stop,
I was on the edge of a cliff.
'Help!'
There were ragged rocks below.
I grabbed onto a rock.
Rocks tumbled down the cliff too.
My heart was pounding like a galloping horse,
What would happen to me?
Would I die?

Abigail Dawson (9)
Grand Avenue Primary School

Limerick

There was a man called Roo,
Who slipped and fell in some poo,
Landed there with a smack,
With a mess up his back,
Why can't dogs just use the loo?

Megan Murphy (10)
Holy Trinity CE Primary School

Limerick

There once was a young man called Mark,
Who went to sleep in a small park,
But the bench was all wet
With cement and he set
And was stuck there until it got dark!

Laurie Grzybkowski (11)
Holy Trinity CE Primary School

A Limerick

A chicken laid a beautiful egg,
It was wet, he dried it on a peg.
It didn't taste nice,
So he had some rice,
The chicken's name was Mrs Mop Meg.

Adam Robinson (11)
Holy Trinity CE Primary School

Cinquain

Bonfire,
Fireworks are loud,
Colours light up the sky,
The bonfire is sparkling red.
Bonfire.

Paul Robinson (11)
Holy Trinity CE Primary School

My Magic Box

(Based on 'Magic Box' by Kit Wright)

I will put in my box . . .

The swish of a silk sari
Shooting silky stars
The killing claws of a crocodile

I will put in my box . . .

A baby with handcuffs
And a policeman with a dummy
A horse who lives under the sea
And a sea horse who lives in a stable
A tiger with spots
And a Dalmatian with stripes.

I will put in my box . . .

A fifth season
A thirteenth month
And an eighth day of the week

My box is fashioned from . . .

Snowflakes
And lush green grass
And polka dots
With diamonds on top
And whispers of leprechauns in the corner
The hinges are the tails of two fishes

I shall build sandcastles in my box
Then smash them down with my sword
After that I shall run to the front of the beach
To swim in the deep blue ocean!

Amber Crisp (10)
Monks Orchard Primary School

The Blitz

Blazing fires constantly burning,
Destruction flowing through the towns.
Shattering windows fall to the ground,
Oh how? How? How?
'Stay calm!' someone shouts,
Nobody listens now.

Heartbroken people fill the town,
As a river of tears start to appear.
Children wailing, screeching, praying,
'Oh why? Why? Why?'
'Help!' someone shouts,
Then a shuffling can be seen.

Burst pipes horribly smelling,
As the smell circles round and round,
Someone coughing, sneezing, choking.
But who? Who? Who?
'Shhh,' someone whispers,
As a song starts to begin.

Oh what has Hitler done?

Catherine Cole (10)
Monks Orchard Primary School

Thunder

T hunder is cracking in the air
H iding under my blue pillow
U nder my bed in my room I can't hear it
N ow how long has it been going on?
D anger is near my house
E very day, it's been five days now
R ain, lightning and thunder.

Kerri Steer (8)
Monks Orchard Primary School

The Blitz

Families running frantically
Back and forth looking for their houses,
People crying for help,
Terrified about what is going on,
The damp smell from pipes being broken,
Big black clouds of smoke in the air,
It's heartbreaking what has happened here,
I can hear the bombs being dropped,
The doodlebugs humming continuously through the air,
Then *bang!*
People are running,
Going to rescue their loved ones,
The planes are flying over our heads,
Hitler is destroying our town.

Priyanka Pau (11)
Monks Orchard Primary School

Will The War Ever Come To An End?

Exploding bombs destroying buildings,
People looking for their children
Just in case they're still alive
And not badly harmed.

Children crying, not knowing what to do,
Sirens screaming twice as loud.
People dying in pain,
Water turning red.

Men hiding everywhere,
Waiting for their enemies to approach.
People hoping their loved ones are still alive.
Fighting until the war comes to an end.

Rebecca Crouch (10)
Monks Orchard Primary School

The Magic Box

(Based on 'Magic Box' by Kit Wright)

I will put in my box . . .

The silk from a spider's web
On a summer's night
The biggest bumps from a camel's back
And a pair of foul-smelling feet

I will put in my box . . .

A policeman robbing a bank
And a robber trying to stop him
A twenty-fifth hour
And a eighth day of the week

I will put in my box . . .

A magical moon that shines during the day
And a super hot sun shining at night

My box is fashioned from snow
And icicles from a snowy cave
Also the smallest stars from outer space.

Ajai Freeman-Lampard (10)
Monks Orchard Primary School

Caroline

C is for Caroline who loves cabbages
A is for apples that I eat
R is for rabbits that I love
O is for oak trees that are very tall
L is for lambs that make jumpers
I is for invisible Caroline
N is for nag that my mum does to me
E is for the eagle that flies over my head.

Caroline Cole (8)
Monks Orchard Primary School

London's Burning

In the dark and sombre sky,
You can hear the German planes dropping bombs as they fly by.

Monstrous flames cover the streets,
Nothing can stop the blazing heat.

Bombs exploding everywhere,
Then silence . . .
Boom!

The ground trembles madly under your feet,
All people do is cry and weep.

Suddenly clouds of poisonous gas fills the air.

Glowing rubble is all over the floor,
Kids in shelters feel quite bored.

Hitler is happy in Germany
And the Blitz has come to be.

Matthew Thomas (10)
Monks Orchard Primary School

Kaashif

K is for Kaashif who is a pupil in Monks Orchard Primary School
A t school I like playing in the adventure playground
A ll the children like the adventure playground
S is for a sensitive Kaashif eating lunch
H is for a home for Kaashif
I f I fell I would not cry!
F is for a full glass of water that Kaashif will drink.

Kaashif Hymabaccus (7)
Monks Orchard Primary School

The Blitz

The doodlebugs whining and then they stop,
Suddenly the ground trembles and windows shatter,
Anti-aircraft guns, blaring bombs raining down on London,
Jerry bombers droning.
Spitfires and Hurricanes,
Machine guns screaming at Meschersmitts and bombers,
Sirens wailing as bombs explode,
Finally it has stopped,
Everyone is hoping their house is still standing,
Everyone is terrified.
Glowing rubble still hot from the fire that was once
Blaring in the night sky,
There is total destruction and everyone is crying
Because their house is no more.

Jack Weeks (11)
Monks Orchard Primary School

Wartime

The ground trembles, more
Dogs barking, suddenly another bomb drops,
I hear babies' cries.
I try to find my gas mask, but it's all smoky,
I know that gas is seeping through the door.
Silence.
I smell burning, I hear whistling,
I see glowing rubble,
I feel the heat.
I hear another bomb exploding,
I hear women screaming,
Then silence.

Paris Blackall (11)
Monks Orchard Primary School

Burning Blitz

I'm laying quietly with my pillow,
In the underground.
I peep through the bottom of a door.
I see lit-up London in pieces.
Glowing rubble,
Demolished buildings.
London is torn apart.

From outside I can hear . . .
Doodlebugs,
Screams of disbelief
And I can feel the ground trembling.
A cloud of gas fills the air,
Bang!
I can hear an engine hovering.
I think to myself,
I'm safe,
Doodlebugs,
London is torn apart.

You think it's an accident,
But Hitler knows what he is doing.
London is torn apart.

Alice Casban (10)
Monks Orchard Primary School

Thunder

T hunder strikes down the street once again.
H undreds of people screaming and shouting.
U nder the shelter everyone, quickly.
N o one's around, they're all in the shelter.
D oors all locked down streets.
E ach and every person down a shelter.
R eaching for food and drinks.

Logan Cohen (8)
Monks Orchard Primary School

My Magic Box

(Based on 'Magic Box' by Kit Wright)

I will put in my box . . .
the swish of a silk sari on a summer night,
the treasure from a glorious golden dragon,
the crazy crack of popping popcorn.

I will put in my box . . .
a pink moon smiling at me,
the blue leaves off an oak tree,
a silky starry sight.

I will put in my box . . .
a 5th season and a black sun,
an 8th day in a week,
the 13th month in a year.

My box is fashioned from the clearest glaciers,
the softest pink petals ever
and golden jewels sprinkled with sweet sugar on the top.

Raeesah Hymabaccus (8)
Monks Orchard Primary School

Foggy

F og is the worst weather to have because in cars or on foot
   you can't see where you are going.
O utside the weather gets worse every second.
G osh, I'm scared, I can't see.
G arden gates cannot be seen in all this dreadful fog.
Y ou should always go prepared for the weather.

Joshua Birchall (8)
Monks Orchard Primary School

The Blitz

The Blitz is here
People running
Babies crying
As the doodlebug whistles by
Silence

Sticky tape on the windows
Fires above the glowing rubble
Smoky ground everywhere
As the doodlebug whistles by
Silence

The wail of the siren cancels out the drone
Of bombers!
Loud gunfire rips the air
As the doodlebug whistles by
Silence

Frightened
Scared
Terrified people
As the ground heaves
People in pain
As the doodlebug whistles by
Silence

Gas filling the air
Smoke in the air
Burning everywhere
As the doodlebug whistles by
Silence

Boom!

Adam Boufenchouche (11)
Monks Orchard Primary School

Blitz

The terror
Bang!
The doodlebugs are whining
Sirens are wailing
People shrieking in terror
Ground breaking explosions
An avalanche of bombs
Silence

Bang!
Petrified people
Wardens chattering nervously
The destruction cast around
Buildings crumbling at the touch
The distant rumbling
The earthquake of the siren

Bang!
The cry of distraught people
Clouds of gas hanging around
Lit up by the explosions
Silence
Maybe the war is over
Or has it just begun?

Chris Harris (11)
Monks Orchard Primary School

Toyanne

T is for table tennis, my best sport.
O is for I am often playing it.
Y is for my yo-yo that I play with.
A is for myself always yo-yoing.
N is for never getting bored.
N is for still never getting bored.
E is for every day I like reading books.

Toyanne Nelson-Thomas (8)
Monks Orchard Primary School

The Blitz

The Blitz was horrible,
People were screaming and crying,
Fear was in the air,
You could hear guns firing from miles away,
Oh why did we go to war?

The Blitz was horrible,
The noise was unbelievable,
Everybody was petrified,
You could see planes fighting from miles away,
Oh why did we go to war?

The Blitz was horrible,
You could feel the ground heave under you,
You couldn't help but feel distraught, terrified,
You were trembling,
Patiently waiting for the next bomb.
Gas was seeping through nearly-destroyed doors,
Slowly, hissing at all times,
But finally they stopped.

Ben Savill (11)
Monks Orchard Primary School

Blitz

Walls crumbling to the hot floor,
Children screaming, bombs dropping.

Smell of smoke, banging bombs,
Babies screaming, feeling terrified as the bombs drop.

Flashes of light,
Mothers wondering if they're going to be alright.

Windows breaking,
Bombs coming down,
People petrified,
Explosions going on.

Jaide Stevenson (10)
Monks Orchard Primary School

Terror

Sirens wailing,
Screams are heard,
Then silence.

Houses destroyed,
Crying is filling the air,
Then silence.

Happiness shattered,
Gunfire is heard,
Then silence.

Craters in the once smooth pavement,
Lives destroyed,
Then fear.

Katie Fanthorpe (11)
Monks Orchard Primary School

The Blitz

Camouflaged
Building
Covered with smoke
Silent blackness

While houses
Are still
Being bombed
Children
Screaming from
Injury

Houses ruined from bombs
Bang!

Shane Nash (10)
Monks Orchard Primary School

The Blitz

Children screaming with fear,
Doodlebugs whining.
Then silence.
Explosion!
Flashes of light,
As the deadly bombs drop,
Shattered windows everywhere,
Then sirens wailing.
Pain all around,
Adults in disbelief,
Everyone scared,
People distraught, sad,
People terrified,
As the ground trembles,
Gas filling the soundless air,
Camouflaged buildings,
Fires burning in the dark silence.
Gloomy streets,
Smoke everywhere,
Glowing rubble,
Wardens chattering
About what's happening,
Exploding bombs making babies cry,
Innocent people being killed
By whining bombs.
Everybody hears the gunfire,
Then *silence.*

Charlotte Hall (11)
Monks Orchard Primary School

My Anderson Shelter

Gunfire
Explosions
Bombs
Then silence
That's what I hear in my Anderson shelter

Gas
Burning
Damp
Smoke
That's what I smell in my Anderson shelter

Nervous
Terrified
Sad
Grim
That's what I feel in my Anderson shelter.

Ben Harper (11)
Monks Orchard Primary School

Blitz

Darkness
Silence
Fear going through
My head
I was in disbelief
Walking on
Shattered glass
Flashes of light
From all directions
Outside you could hardly breathe
Gas running up your nose
Constantly
Mothers weeping, babies dead
It was catastrophic.

Tom Cully (10)
Monks Orchard Primary School

My Chicken Sandwich

Enormous, fat, juicy, flat sandwich.
A big Chinese dragon with fireworks exploding,
Fiery flames,
Sweet tomatoes,
Rich, tasty, fresh, glorious, succulent chicken.
Mouth-watering, tongue sizzling,
Royal chicken in a limey sauce,
Crunchy bread.
I want more,
I feel ecstatic!
My tummy is waiting for
More!
More!
More!
Begging for only a little bite to eat.
I have the next bite,
So glorious,
My tummy will be so relieved
That it will want more,
More!
More!

Gobi Varatha-Rajan (8)
Monks Orchard Primary School

Fish And Chips

As I look at my food,
I know I am not allowed to gobble it down my throat,
When I look at it I can hear it saying,
Eat me!
It reminds me of people surrounding an Atlantic island,
Jostling for my food,
I want to gobble it down my throat forever,
I feel like I've got all the glory in the world.

Kieran Hendry-Hall (8)
Monks Orchard Primary School

White Chocolate

Long, silky, polished
Chunk of snow,
Swifting through the air,
Cold
With a slight crunch,
I need more!
My tummy is trembling,
More!
More!
More!
Afterwards there's a milky taste
In my empty mouth,
I'm relieved,
I've eaten it.

Andrew Callam (8)
Monks Orchard Primary School

Omelette

Round and round
Like a bouncy basketball,
As huge as my brother's head
Waiting to burst,
Cannonballs dropping
From the dangerous sky,
Smells delicious,
Taste buds ready to burst,
Juicy, succulent piglets,
More!
Glorious food!

Stephanie Ockwell (9)
Monks Orchard Primary School

Home-Made Steak Pie!

Lumps of tender meat
Encased in soft, crusty pastry and gravy,
Asian fireballs,
Flying into the dark watery hole,
Steaming beefy sauce,
I can't resist.
I'm weak,
It's on my brass fork,
I see tasty clouds,
It slides into the empty dustbin,
Burning, scorching in my watery mouth,
A drink will spoil it,
More!
More!
More!
Sensational food!

Lauren Trout (9)
Monks Orchard Primary School

Spicy Chicken

Like a burning, crispy, hot potato,
Sizzling on the dancing fire grill,
Glowing, fiery chicken breast,
Meaty, chewy, sensational, tropical crispiness,
Sweet, fragrant aroma,
Steamy and irresistible,
My mouth waters like a streaming river,
I feel like I'm going to *die!*
If I don't have that succulent deep fried taste,
More!

Nekkita Hollett (8)
Monks Orchard Primary School

Nuts!

Skinny, round, like an oval,
Baby rocks,
Spicy and crunchy bars,
Salty lava rocks,
Waiting to enter my dark cave,
Waiting,
Begin!
End!
Hunger!
Just like my nan's Spanish omelette.
Relaxed!
Finally
Done!
Relief!
More!

Samantha Ray (8)
Monks Orchard Primary School

The Blitz

Ruins of houses lay still in flames,
Terrified children, wailing babies.
Chaos, panic, clouds of smoke,
Disaster strikes once again.

People lay still, dead frozen on cold, hard ground,
People's lives have gone,
But they will live in Heaven forever.

People crying, 'Please stop.'
Why start war? Will it never end?
Who will save us now?

Roxann Johnson (11)
Monks Orchard Primary School

Curry Goat

Lots of spices and lumpy like lots of stones on my plate,
White paper all cut up,
Lots of lumpy mud all splashed on my plate,
It smells like the fresh new mint plant in my garden,
Mouth-watering, what a rumbly belly!
There's never too much of it,
Chewy like chewing gum,
I want a drink, it's so spicy,
It's spicy like a lump of pepper and mustard,
I'm hungry for more,
Yum! Yum!
Scrum! Scrum!
Food in my tum!

Kane Lawe (9)
Monks Orchard Primary School

Chicken Korma

Smooth, slimy, dark yellow,
Creamy, shiny sauce.
Bumpy, sweet, chewy chicken,
Steaming chillis in the lumpy,
Sweet rocks covered with hairs on top.
I'm desperate!
I want to take the first bite!
It's slithering down my tube
Throat like a snake!
I want some more!

Danielle Addison (9)
Monks Orchard Primary School

Duck!

Fat, tender, juicy,
Sweet and sour sauce,
Waiting to burn in
My caved mouth.
Enormous mountains covered
In thick, gigantic, slippery, brown mud.
Hissing like
Sausages sizzling on the
Searching, scorching,
Magnificent grill.
I'm desperate,
Empty, bottomless hole
Begging for emergency escape,
Crispy!
Saucy!
Delicious!
Mouth-watering!
Glorious!
More!

Anna-Marie Hart (9)
Monks Orchard Primary School

Chicken Curry

Rocks covered in lava,
White pieces of broken statue.
Burning, fiery rocks waiting
To disintegrate and melt.
Chicken curry sauce!
I'm desperate and starving,
Sweet, juicy, wonderful!
My tongue is all watery,
Crispy, smooth boulders,
Diving through the hole.
More!

Anthony Young (9)
Monks Orchard Primary School

Chicken Korma

Covered in red sauce
White, juicy rice
Like fat lumps of chalky rocks
Waiting to be chewed
Hot, red tastiness
Sizzling on my plate
I'm desperate!
The spicy aroma
Burns my suffering tongue
The mouth-watering moment has begun
At last!
Fire dancing on my caged lips
Chunks of steaming chicken
Fall into the furious cave
More!
More!
More!
Settled relief.

Atlanta Gunstone (8)
Monks Orchard Primary School

Jerk Chicken And Rice

Brown chicken
Like dark, hard wood.
Smells like a smoky barbecue.
My heart beats fast
Like a stampede of elephants.
I feel excited.
Hard, crispy juices.
Relaxed.
More!
More!
More!

Klavel Millanaise (8)
Monks Orchard Primary School

Jerk Chicken

Gigantic piece of slobbering meat,
Sizzling, burning, volcanic chilli lava
Like a pint of juicy gravy
From the supermarket.
Red, flaming hot sauce over my jerk chicken.
Smoky, garlicky, crispiness hissing
On the sparkling, scorching gravy,
Hisssss!
I feel a piece that tender,
Tastes like tender, roasted turkey,
I need more!

Jobi Freeman-Lampard (9)
Monks Orchard Primary School

Chocolate

Very dark brown with lumps,
It smells like cola,
Before the first bite it makes me feel hungry,
It tastes soft and creamy in my mouth,
Chocolate!
When I look at it
My mouth begins to water,
It's all gone now,
I want more!

Adam Field (9)
Monks Orchard Primary School

Burger And Chips

Juicy worms,
Salty chips,
Slippery, tender burger,
Greasy meat just from the
Blazing, fiery oven.
I'm desperate!
Am I dreaming?
Crunchy chips,
Scrummy burger!
Delicious!

Jessica Mothersole (9)
Monks Orchard Primary School

Roast Chicken

Crunchy, soft chicken,
Smooth delightful gravy,
Enormous sloping hill in the flaming oven,
Steaming fire with garlicky spices,
Licking my lips!
I need to fill my empty hole
With ginger pepper!
I really want . . .
More!

Alexis Loizou (8)
Monks Orchard Primary School

Fish And Chips

They look like little rectangles
Lying beside a round face.
The smell of the vinegar makes me desperate to eat,
My tummy is rumbling,
I can't wait to eat my fish and chips.

Daniel Peter Bennet-Williams (8)
Monks Orchard Primary School

Lightning

L is for lightning swooping down hitting trees.
I n the dark sky lightning comes by.
G o away, go away, please come another day!
H is for horror of the terrifying lightning, hear it strike again.
T is for thunder swooping by.
N ow the town is neat, now it is messy.
I see lightning coming by, what are we to do?
N ever go outside unless it is clear.
G is for a giant lightning bolt striking at your house.

Jonathan Mollah (8)
Monks Orchard Primary School

Wedges

Potato with a bit of spice that's crispy.
Smells like potato being mashed with butter.
Great inside my tummy.
I'm desperate for food.
It tastes mouth-watering
Going down my throat.
Feels great.
Shaped like a banana.
I want more, more, more!

Kirsty Brooks (8)
Monks Orchard Primary School

Rain

R is for rain that shoots down.
A is for art that rain creates.
I is for I can see the rain.
N is for it has nearly stopped.

Victor Dokubo (8)
Monks Orchard Primary School

Katharine!

K is for Katharine who likes to do maths.
A is for apple, yummy for me.
T is for teddy, soft and cuddly.
H is for horse, lovely and furry.
A is for ABC which I like to sing.
R is for rabbit, cute as can be.
I is for ice cream lovely to eat.
N is for nuggets, delicious for me.
E is for exploring which I love to do.

Katharine Semple (7)
Monks Orchard Primary School

My Favourite Food Is Turkey

Brown, crispy and soft
Oily like a shiny metal handle
Meaty gravy and juicy meat
More!
I want more tasty turkey
Crunchy skin tastes delicious
Yum!
Full up and can't eat anymore.

Travis Jones (8)
Monks Orchard Primary School

One Day

I went to a shop one day,
But then I saw someone that did not pay.
I dialled 999,
So the man got a fine.
He later went to jail
And of course, looking rather pale.
He's been in jail for 6 years now,
All because of long ago.
A crime he had committed,
But now he's paid the price.
However, now it will haunt him for the rest of his life.
When he went to jail,
He missed his child's birth
And now his wife thinks he's the worst person on Earth.
He is all alone
And hasn't even got a home.

You might think it's cool,
But at the end, you'll just look like a fool.

Kayleigh Bennett (11)
Mytchett Primary School

Anger

Anger is when my little sister turns the television over
When I'm watching my favourite programme - The Simpsons.
Anger is when my auntie eats all the chocolates
In the cupboard when I really want one.
Anger is when I miss a party because I'm sick.
Anger is when I'm not allowed outside
When all my friends are out.
Anger is when my mum promised to take me shopping
And then she goes to her friend's house.
Anger is a volcano erupting in my head.
Anger is a raging bull inside me.

Jodie Stevens (11)
Mytchett Primary School

Theft Poem

I'm looking around a shop,
I'm bored and I'm thirsty.
I see a can of Coke.

Should I take it or should I not?

I'm getting closer now,
My mouth is dry and I'm hungry.
I also see a packet of crisps.

Should I take it or should I not?

I look left and right,
I can't hear anything.
I don't think there is anyone about.

Should I take it or should I not?

And now I'm in a jail cell.

Should I have taken it?

No, I should not.

Oliver Surey (11)
Mytchett Primary School

Bullying

It comes out from behind the corner,
It picks me up by my side.
It throws me on the floor,
It makes me want to cry.

It makes me feel frustrated,
It makes me not want to play.
It makes me feel intimidated,
I need to get away.

David Morgan (11)
Mytchett Primary School

I Wanna Be A Superstar

I wanna be a superstar,
I wanna ride a convertible car.
I wanna stop every war,
I wanna own a chocolate store.
I wanna have a Persian cat,
I wanna have a cowgirl's hat.
I wanna be a great singer,
I wanna be a British Olympic winner.
I wanna have a pink limousine,
I wanna get rid of all the mean.
I wanna have my own range of clothes,
I wanna have three fashion shows.
I wanna be the most popular child,
I wanna have a monkey which is wild.
On second thoughts,
Now, let me see,
I think I'm better off as me.

Francesca Reah (10)
Mytchett Primary School

Theft

I'm sitting on a park bench, *bored,*
I don't know what to do.
In my mind, I can hear my friends telling me what I should do.
To be one of the gang, I have to go to steal
A chocolate bar and a fancy coat.
It's so unfair,
But they're still there giving me this awkward dare.
Shall I do it?
Shall I not?
I have to, they're the only friends I've got.

Lucy Smith (10)
Mytchett Primary School

Theft

It was only a can of Coke, is that such a crime?
My mate down the road, he stole a bottle of wine,
Now I've got a fine of 109.

I went into a shop,
I just couldn't stop.
I only stole a lime,
But someone called 999.
They caught me
And now I can't have a cup of tea
Because they threw me in a cell,
It's like being in Hell.

So don't steal, it is bad,
They'll put you in jail
And you'll just end up feeling really sad.

Peter Hammond (10)
Mytchett Primary School

Fear

Fear is footsteps following me down a dark alleyway
With nothing behind you.
Fear is a hand grabbing my shoulder in a power cut.
Fear is when my family choke and haunt me for it.
Fear is when I'm trapped and you're frozen with fear
And someone's breathing on your neck.
Fear is being in a tomb with coffins and skeletons.
Fear is being in a forest with people with rope around
Their necks hanging off the tree branches.
Fear is the howl of a werewolf in a foggy, marshy meadow.

William Smith (11)
Mytchett Primary School

Theft

It all started when I was 18,
I went to the shop and stole an ice cream.
In the beginning I was really cool,
Now I know I was just a fool.
Two days later, I was back at the shop,
The thrill of the steal, I couldn't stop.
The rush and the buzz, it was great,
I knew stealing would be my fate.
This was the last thing I thought,
Just before I was tragically caught.
7 long years I spent in jail,
Without one single day of bail.
I see my family fill with hate,
So much for stealing being great.

Andrew Lockwood (11)
Mytchett Primary School

Fear Is . . .

Fear is seeing the candyman in the mirror,
Holding his dagger and seeing it shimmer.
Fear is when there is a power cut
And the lights are getting dimmer.
Fear is someone stalking me,
Constantly, day and night.
Fear is being crushed by a bulldozer
On a busy building site.

Felipe Paz-Howlett (11)
Mytchett Primary School

The Bully

It makes me feel as sad as watching a
Family member die in my arms.

Wherever I turn, he is there.

He is tormenting me, day and night.

He physically strikes, leaving me with bruises.

He is such a pest, why won't he give it a rest?

When he sees me bleed,
He charges at me like a bull.

I feel like the prey and he is the predator,
He continuously strikes me with his mighty lion's paw.

He is such a pest, he is such a pest,
Why won't he give it a rest?

Sean Ratcliffe (11)
Mytchett Primary School

Bullying

It tries to scare me with its frightening look.
It terrorises my day, I wish it would just go away.
Every corner I turn, I'm there feeling burnt, won't this bully learn?
I feel I'm being haunted, every day and night.
I feel I'm up against a really big fight.
It makes me so scared, I have to turn on the light.
It hurts me in a nasty way, won't he ever go away?
When I say leave me alone, he still follows me home.

Daniela Campitelli (11)
Mytchett Primary School

The Singo

The Singo,
The Singo,
Its eyes are like bingo,
Its blood is bluish,
Its voice is hoarse and bubbish,
Its tentacles are crummy,
Slimy, bubbly and scrummy!
Its lips are hungry, blubbery,
Rubbery, gulky, and slobbery.
The Singo,
The Singo,
I saw it just a minute ago,
Last night, it was in the living room,
Tonight, it is in my bedroom!
As it was skulking round
I looked up and turned around,
Then it saw me and I said, 'Help!'
Then it gulped me up
And said, 'That helped!'

Nicole Noonan (10)
Mytchett Primary School

Fear Is . . .

Fear is a haunted house in an eerie wood.
Fear is a spider creeping up your leg.
Fear is when you hear something in your bed.
Fear is a bee stinging you while you are playing.
Fear is seeing a fin peer up while you are swimming in the sea.

Christian James (11)
Mytchett Primary School

The Vamblimbo

The Vamblimbo,
The Vamblimbo,
Its teeth are like knives,
Its eyes are like disco balls that glisten in the night,
Its tentacles are like sausages, smelly sausages at that,
Its voice is like hammers banging, waking me up at night.

The Vamblimbo,
The Vamblimbo,
It's in my room tonight,
I'm scared it will pop out from under my bed
And give me a bad fright!
I think I'd better turn the light on
Or it could come out and bite.

Nicola Salmon (9)
Mytchett Primary School

Why? Why? Why?

Why? Why? Why
Did I do it?
It was only a measly can of Coke.
Why? Why? Why
Did I do it? It was only a little joke.

No! No! No!
I thought I was cool.
No! No! No!
I now realise I'm a fool.

Don't! Don't! Don't
Put me in a cell!
Don't! Don't! Don't
Call my mum
Because she will only scream and yell!

Ryan George (11)
Mytchett Primary School

The Monster I Got Rid Of

Beneath my bed, a monster dwells,
It gives off lots of rancid smells.

His warty face is really manky
And for his nose, he needs a hanky.

His skin is green and blubbery,
His lips are red and rubbery.

His arms are big and scaly,
His voice is loud and waily.

When monsters spoil your bedtime rest,
I'll tell you the plan that works the best.

Just tell that thing from under your bed,
To go and eat your sis instead.

Joseph Bartlett (10)
Mytchett Primary School

Fear Is . . .

Fear is an evil dream, which drowns you in horror.
Fear is a black hole with no return.
Fear is being trapped in a room with all your worst nightmares.
Fear is a sinister demon which stalks you every night and day.
Fear is a bloodshot creature which lives under your bed.
Fear is being trapped in a room with an enormous, venomous snake.
Fear is a lifelong threat, which never goes away.

Sam Kocher (10)
Mytchett Primary School

What's That In There?

What that in there?
What's that wiggling?
What's that wiggling down in the black
Of this frozen, dark, damp, dangerous cave?

Is it Marallo?
The lime lizard with twenty
Turquoise heads
With teeth that instantly snap like a trap?

What's that in there?
What's that wiggling?
What's that wiggling down in the black
Of this frozen, dark, damp, dangerous cave?

Is it Barron?
The slimy, silver, slippery snake
With spiky horns all over his body?

What's that in there?
What's that wiggling?
What's that wiggling down in the black
Of this frozen, dark, damp, dangerous cave?

Is it Larissa?
The girl who died
And haunts the cave
With hypnotising eyes
That could kill you in a second?

Kirsty Whiting (9)
Mytchett Primary School

What's That Down There?

What's that down there crawling under my bed?
It's the spotty, smelly, stomping monster
That strolls in the night.

What's that down there crawling under my bed?
It's the blubbery, bumpy, booming monster
That bangs in the night.

What's that down there crawling under my bed?
It's the scaly, slithery, stinky monster
That shouts in the night.

What's that down there crawling under my bed?
It's the blotchy, bony, bleachy monster
That bites in the night.

Daisy Ward (9)
Mytchett Primary School

Gut Cruncher

He's slimy, he's green, he smells of rotten weeds.
If you go near, you'll have nightmares for a year.
If you go around, be sure to check the ground,
For this monster will pound if you walk around.

He's spiky, he's mean, he's gloomy red and misty green.
When you enter his cave, you'll be sliced and sacrificed.
You'll be clustered like mustard and your bones will be fractured.
He's like hard rock and slimy PVA glue.

If you've heard him, you wouldn't have a clue what to do.

Riccardo Campitelli (9)
Mytchett Primary School

The Liverwood

The Liverwood! The Liverwood!
You would never get there, if you could!
If you could, you never should!

His tail swishes, slashes and sways!
Get near and you must get away!
You must retreat from it,
Its jaw is like a giant pit!

Don't tell it a lie
Or you'll be a person pie!
Get away! Get away!
Or you won't see another day!

It's worse than losing your fie!
The minimum is that you'll die!
His real name is Stef
And you'll meet his best friend, Death!

Jacob Owen (9)
Mytchett Primary School

The Escaping Dragon

I saw a huge dragon in a cave,
His teeth were so white,
He gave me a fright.

I was taking him to safety,
But that made him hate me.

I got him in a cage,
But he got in a rage.

His mouth filled with fire,
Which burnt the wire.

The dragon escaped,
With a smile on his face,
Never again to be traced.

Michael Duncan (10)
Mytchett Primary School

Things That Do Stuff When They Want To!

If you see a giant frog
Looking for a fight,
Smash the light bulbs, run at the wall,
Pick your nose with a kite.

Stick bacon on your eyes with snot,
Lean upon your bed,
Stick a bogey upon your face,
Hit yourself in the head.

If randomly the bogeyman
Pays you a quick visit,
Rub chocolate spread around your ears
And search your hair for nits.

Tip green paint all over your head,
Pour jam down your pants,
Turn around and shake your bottom,
Then eat a load of ants.

If you smell the Blaa-Blaa
Underneath the shed,
Scribble upon your big fat face,
Paint your fingers red.

Poke yourself in the eyes with might,
Boil an egg very quick,
Pull your hair as hard as you can,
Leap around with a stick.

Liam Sanders (10)
Mytchett Primary School

If You're Scared Of Monsters . . .

If you see the Dendigo
Skulking in the night,
Shut all the doors and windows,
Cross your fingers tight.
Stand upon your head,
Count one, two, three,
Jump backwards in the sea.

If you hear the Rainbowcoot
Whilst walking in the park,
Pick up the nearest big, long stick
And run to some place dark.
Put your head between your legs,
Turn three times upon your heel
And quietly utter a high-pitched squeal.

If you smell the Balencee
When you're sitting on the loo,
Make a quiet clucking noise,
Then utter 'dodolo'.
Paint your face with blue spots,
Circle them with big dots.

Rachel Franklin-Heys (9)
Mytchett Primary School

Bullying

It chases me every day, non-stop.
It is like cat and mouse.
Everywhere I go, it is there.
I feel like a punch bag, day and night.
Can't it just go away?
Why can't it leave me alone? Why? Why? Why?
Its red eyes are petrifying.
I have to see it day and night.
I scream when I see it in my dreams.
I feel like my life is so empty, all because of it.

Chris Green (10)
Mytchett Primary School

The Flompolomb

The Flompolomb,
The Flompolomb,
Its tummy is very scrummy!
Its blood is red and yellowish!
Its voice is low and bellowish!
Its fingers are bony and dry!
Its lips are slimy and blubbery!
Its body is spotty and fat,
Leathery, sucky and rubbery!

The Flompolomb,
The Flompolomb!
It travels all around the world,
Last night it lurked in Flump Typhoon,
Now it's in your perfect bedroom!
As you are sleeping in your bed . . .
It will gobble you up and you'll be dead!

Shane Dunn (10)
Mytchett Primary School

Bullying

It comes every day,
Just to get me.

It ruins my best days
And haunts my darkest nights.

I have a fear,
One day it will get me.

When it runs, it's like a swift cheetah,
When I run, I'm just like a startled mouse.

I don't have any friends, although I did,
I'll do anything to get some.

Joel Pace (11)
Mytchett Primary School

Monster Mayhem

What's in the cave?
What's that moving?
What's that moving down in the dark of the icy, black, wet cave?

Is it Crash?
That terrifying black monster
Who lurks around when it's pitch-black,
In the silver light of the moon
And his head covered in 200 spikes,
As well as his head, the smell is deadly.

What's in the cave?
What's that moving?
What's that moving down in the dark of the icy, black, wet cave?

Is it Phoney Phantom?
That slimy, slithery ghost
Of a girl who died in this crumbly, sticky cave.
Every night you hear her moans
That sound like the howling of a deadly, ferocious wolf.

What's in the cave?
What's that moving?
What's that moving down in the dark of the icy, black, wet cave?

Is it Proculer?
That black, huge, spiky monster.
Its roar sounds like an earthquake
And it smells like manky cheese.
Its rough, gooey skin flakes off.

Charlotte Warrender (10)
Mytchett Primary School

The Spiderhorn

The Spiderhorn!
The Spiderhorn!
Its skin is lemon-yellow and torn!
Its lips are ice-white
And it smells of Marmite!
Its hair is bogey-green and scrubby,
Its toenails are inky-black and grubby!
Its voice is croaky and hoarse
And its palms are rancid and coarse!
Its tongue is blubbery!
Flubbery!
Slubbery!
Rubbery!

The Spiderhorn!
The Spiderhorn!
I wish it had never been born!
It rips you apart
And takes out your heart!
Last night it was in Peru,
Tonight it will crawl out of your loo!
While you are snoring in bed,
It will devour you, like it hasn't been fed!
You scream!
It tears!
It wallows!
The rest is mostly gulps and swallows!

Louis Browne (9)
Mytchett Primary School

What's That?

What's that down there?
What's that creeping around?
What's that creeping around, way down there
In this pitch-black, breezy hole of a cave?

Is it Dingle Dog?
That silly, backstabbing dog,
With a long, lightning, green, scaly tail
That flicks every second,
Darting about in the silver moonlight.
Its skin is like leather and sounds like a whip.

What's that way down there?
What's that creeping around?
What's that creeping around, way down there
In this pitch-black, breezy hole of a cave?

Is it Yerepities?
That whispering ghost that lives under the
Mist of the underground lake,
Who died from an earthquake.
Every night you hear her moans
That echo all around the crispy, crummy cave.

What's that way down there?
What's that creeping around?
What's that creeping around, way down there
In this pitch-black, breezy hole of a cave?

Is it Phanty?
That cackling, black, phoney phantom
Who died in this very cave,
With a slippery wisp of anyone who entered
And a hundred clippy claws that can rip your heart out.
It has a smell that wanders
Around the crummy cave,
A smell that you can never get out of your nose.

What's that way down there?
What's that creeping around?
What's that creeping around, way down there
In this pitch-black, breezy hole of a cave?
Well, if you want to find out
You'll have to go down there
And figure it out!

Emma Warrender (10)
Mytchett Primary School

What's In There?

What's in there?
What's in there?
What's lurking down there?
What's in the dark, damp, spooky cave?

Is it Nightmare?
That walking headless beast which could kill you
With its big hands which wrap around you and crushes you.

What's in there?
What's lurking down there?
What's in the dark, damp, spooky cave?

Is it Crusher?
That old, mad man who died in an abandoned house
And his cry is as loud as a thunderstorm?

What's in there?
What's lurking down there?
What's in the dark, damp, spooky cave?

Is it Scarecrow?
That man stuffed up who's itchy and stitched up tightly
But just because he's a scarecrow doesn't mean
He can't kill you with his hands,
Down in the dark, damp, spooky cave.

Robert Brady (9)
Mytchett Primary School

Monsters In The Dark

Messy monster,
Funny monster,
Jumping monster,
Lives in a deep, dark puzzle of a cave.

The messy monster
Is as big as an elephant,
It has silver, slithery skin,
It lives in the deep, dark puzzle of a cave.

Messy monster,
Funny monster,
Jumping monster,
Lives in a deep, dark puzzle of a cave.

The funny monster
Is as small as a mouse,
It has a banana-shaped bunk bed,
It lives in a deep, dark puzzle of a cave.

Messy monster,
Funny monster,
Jumping monster,
Lives in a deep, dark puzzle of a cave.

The jumping monster
Is as leapy as a kangaroo,
It has pinky-purpley poo,
It lives in a deep, dark puzzle of a cave.

Messy monster,
Funny monster,
Jumping monster,
Lives in a deep, dark puzzle of a cave.

Georgina Cooper (9)
Mytchett Primary School

The Big Green Monster

The monster is green,
The biggest ever seen.

He was very keen
To keep himself clean
And really quite mean.

Chomping here,
Chomping there,
Galloping,
Galloping
Everywhere!

He likes to eat meat,
Especially as a treat.
So if you should ever meet the monster,
You may become the treat.
Yum!

Christine Pryce (9)
Mytchett Primary School

The Deofant

There's a monster in my bedroom, I'll tell you what he's like.
The monster in my bedroom is bright red and green.
The monster in my bedroom smells like a garbage chute,
He is not very clean.

The monster in my bedroom has eyes like ice,
The monster in my bedroom is not very nice.
The monster in my bedroom is tall and slimy,
The monster in my bedroom is getting closer and I'm dead.

Rebecca Steele (9)
Mytchett Primary School

Monsters Scare You

Monsters, monsters, monsters
Really scare you.
They live in a gloomy cave
And come charging up to you.

Is it a Sprout Guzzler?
The long, slimy, smooth tail,
With its bulging green, gooey eyes.

Monster, monsters, monsters
Really scare you.
They live in a gloomy cave
And come slithering up to you.

Is it a Plamglotis?
The long, sticky arms sticking in his enormous mouth,
With gappy teeth and a lumpy tongue.

Monsters, monsters, monsters
Really scare you.
They live in a gloomy cave
And come wobbling up to you.

Catherine Vass (10)
Mytchett Primary School

Fear

Fear is a scary nightmare that is always with you.
Fear is like being trapped in a room filled with hairy, creepy spiders.
Fear is as scary as being bullied and not being able to tell anyone.
Fear is as frightening as being held underwater, gasping for air.
Fear is as scary as being in a room filled with wasps
                            stinging me every second.

Thomas Fyvie (10)
Mytchett Primary School

Is That A Monster Down There?

Is that a monster down there
In that dark cave?
What could it be?

Is it the chilly, cold, ice monster
Or is it the chubby, spotty, noisy,
Stinky, frosty monster?

Whatever one it is, it shall eat you
In one second and these monsters
Smell like body odour.

Even if you were six miles away
It would whizz past you like a man
On a motorbike, so . . .

Is that a monster down there
In that dark cave?
What could it be?

Sian Poulter (9)
Mytchett Primary School

Christmas Time

Racing through the snow, Jack Frost is chasing me.
Dashing through a blizzard.
I do not dare to look behind.
Icicles spiking into my back.
A shrill fear is racing through my body.
I skid across the sheet ice.
I feel chilly and crisp.
My toes are going numb.
In the air it is Arctic, polar and I feel raw.
Crisp, cold and chilly,
This is winter's own fault.

Hannah Kessler (10)
Old Vicarage School

Summer Days

Summer days bright and busy,
Cars go past without stopping,
Back seat children arguing,
Looking forward to arriving.

Summer days,
Cool down in the sea,
Dive . . . *splash!*
Scream with excitement.

Summer days,
Sunbathe in the garden,
Buzz, sting, 'Oww!'
Wasps stinging.

Summer days,
Strawberries growing around me,
Start to eat them, mouths get sticky,
Wash face to cool down.

Scarlett Dockery (7)
Old Vicarage School

Dreamland

Clouds settled on the rolling mountains,
Birds sang in the trees,
Mist dusted the lush green hills
And plants swayed in the breeze.

The dimming sun,
The glistening dew,
Pink and white butterflies
Came into view.

Swans on the lake buried heads in feathers
And ducklings huddled close,
The sun prepared for another day ahead
And dreamland went to bed.

Polly Lamming (9)
Old Vicarage School

Winter Days

Winter days
Cold and quiet
Night is filled with snowflakes
Not a car to be seen.

Winter days
Christmas is coming
Putting up the tree
Santa is coming.

Winter days
Sitting round the fire
Warming our toes
On a cold winter's night.

Winter days
Round the table
Eating chicken
And chocolate pudding!

Winter days
Skating on the rink
Wearing my new boots
Trying hard not to fall.

Pippa Tatton-Brown (7)
Old Vicarage School

Mystery Cat

Soft slinking round and about,
Black mystery in and out,
In the garden, in the house,
Maybe even chasing a mouse.
The cat of mystery, the cat of sly,
Everywhere you go he is watching you
With his mysterious cat eye.

Taylor Hawkins (10)
Old Vicarage School

Winter Days

Snow is falling,
Children shout, 'Hooray!'
Everybody rush outside
And it's time to play.

Children building snowmen,
Adults shovelling snow.
People slowly trudging
In deep, crunchy snow.

Wrapped up for tobogganing,
Squealing with delight,
Plodding up the hill,
Everything's sparkly white.

Children crying, 'Oh no,
The snowman is melting!'
Icicles drip away,
Last snowballs pelting.

Lottie Till (8)
Old Vicarage School

Winter

The old branches ache,
The tree stands naked,
Frozen, sad and bare.
Deep underground is where the spirit lies
And waits for the returning sun,
To wake him from his long woody sleep.

Alice Hewitt (10)
Old Vicarage School

Winter Days

Winter days, fine and white
Snowy grounds of crystals shining bright
Flurries and breezes going fast
Crunch! Crunch! Crunch! Sparkling silver glass

Winter days, fun and exciting
Hoping Santa Claus brings many lovely things
When you wake up, what do you find?
Lots of gifts glistening fine

Winter days, the white snow looks so nice
Skate, skate, skate on the very slippery ice
Ski with my dad, going very fast
Looking for Mum who always comes last

Winter days, have snowball fights
Oh my gosh, it is 8 o'clock at night
Snuggle in bed, nice and tight
Dream of more snow, turn off the light.

Grace Morrison (7)
Old Vicarage School

Fire

As I watch the fire burn,
I see dancers twist and turn.
I see their hair flash like a dart,
I see them move faster than my heart.
Their clothes are made of blue violet fire
And the smoke dances higher and higher.
Sparks fly out before my eyes
And with a final flicker the fire dies.

Rose Fisher (10)
Old Vicarage School

Winter Days

Winter days
City silent
Not a car to be heard
All calm and quiet

Winter days
Snowflakes falling
Shivering in the cold
Icicles like crystals

Winter days
Looking beautiful
Ice all slippery
Frost all crunchy

Winter days
All crisp and cold
Cuddled up on my bed
About to fall asleep.

Tara Cobham (7)
Old Vicarage School

Secrets

My sister has a secret,
I know it.
Every day she buys a Mars bar at the sweet shop.
She is not allowed.
I have gained £7.32 this week.
Blackmail is not allowed either.

I have lost £8.22 this week.
I happen to buy wine gums every day,
I am not allowed.
Teacher said to use strong adjectives
The one I use for my sister is anger -
If that is an adjective.
Oh, how I miss my wine gums!

Caroline Anapol (9)
Old Vicarage School

Summer Days

Summer days,
Flowers blossom,
Sparkling butterflies,
Sweltering sun.

Summer days,
Warm nights,
Thin sheets,
Sun bright.

Summer days,
Gleaming water,
Short sleeve shirts,
Lying in the sun.

Summer days,
Buttercups growing,
Gardeners mowing,
Knowing summer's nearly going.

Miranda Burrows (8)
Old Vicarage School

Fire

It starts as a slither,
Then moves fast to find food.
It hunts for people,
Animals, anything it can find.
When it finds what it wants,
It wraps its hot tail round it
And bites a boiling burn into its skin.
It waits silently watching its prey
Melt into its mouth,
Then it gets bigger and bigger,
Its beautiful colours spreading
Across the land
And then it dies down,
Like a snake slithering off.

Sophie Marr (10)
Old Vicarage School

Summer Days

Summer days, flowers blooming,
Flowers bright and colourful,
Trees with blossom, geraniums,
Wonderful fuchsias spreading their petals.

Summer days, garden beautiful,
Rainbow shining in the sky,
Bumblebees buzzing round and round,
Garden wet and dry.

Summer days people busy,
Packing cases, grabbing hats,
Summer holidays they will go on,
Golden sand and lazy days.

Summer days, children paddling,
Ocean blue and foamy white,
Catching fish in shiny nets,
Barbecues under starry nights.

Saskia Gibbs (7)
Old Vicarage School

Anger

Anger is a blazing fire
It is red and hard
Once you are trapped in anger you cannot get out
It comes from the underworld Devil
Do not go near it or it will bolt you down
Beware, it starts off small but it will grow wild.

Saskia de Jager (11)
Old Vicarage School

Winter Days

Winter days
Cosy nights
Icy roads
Snowflakes dance

Winter days
Crackling fire
Sparkling cobwebs
Glistening frost
On sleepy cars

Winter days
Owls hooting
Pigeons cooing
Blackbirds gone

Winter days
Stockings hung
Waiting for St Nick to come
Sleeping in the morning.

Annabel Marr (7)
Old Vicarage School

Anger

Anger in my eyes is a dark heart breaking blackness,
A house burning in front of my eyes, stinging till it hurts,
Weak, fragile till this monster comes out,
Lungs ache from breathing in fiery smoke,
Mother's hair is soft for the last time,
I fall to my feet like a sickly horse,
Anger has taken me, do not follow my path,
End will be near for those who love.

Caitlin Robbins (11)
Old Vicarage School

Sleek And Black

Sleek and black, it leaves no shadow
As it scampers through the bushes
Into the dark night sky.

Descending through the neighbourhood gardens
Pouncing on prey whenever it dares
To attend its presence.

Aquamarine eyes glare through the hedge
As a mouse appears
From the dazzling darkness of the night.

All is quiet as the brave, cunning animal
Walks through the black veil of shadows.

There's a slight creak as it claws over
The broken fence and there it sleeps
Till night comes once again.

Maya Chaldecott (10)
Old Vicarage School

My Sister, Lola

Dawn approaches,
The night has become weak,
As a red sky returns - shepherds' warning begins.

She brightens up the day, with the colour of peach,
But acts like a jaguar when she is feeling blue.
Her voice is as sweet as a piccolo.

Her eyes are as green as emeralds.
Her cheeks as soft as a cub's new fur
With lips as red as the rose.
For her mind, it was blessed with a daffodil,
That will guide her for evermore.
I know she will have many great adventures,
This is to you.

My sister, Lola.

Ines Anderson (10)
Old Vicarage School

Winter Days

Winter days, summer's gone,
Icicles hanging, candles shone,
Glistening snowflakes, slippery roads,
Santa's carrying heavy loads.

Winter days, summer's gone,
Shadows falling on the sun,
Lights on early, coats on tight,
Carol concert is tonight.

Winter days, summer's gone,
Flowers closing, animals dozing,
Glistening snowflakes fall around,
Sparkling jewels on the ground.

Winter days, summer's gone,
Crystal clear ice rinks with skaters on,
Home to cosy fires, hot chocolate,
Muffins for tea, I hope one's for me.

Anna McGrane (7)
Old Vicarage School

Greed

Greed guzzles like a hungry pig,
It takes over the warmest of places,
The taste of greed is cold and unwanted.
It closes around you like a cage,
The emotion jumps from one person to another,
Spreading its envy.

It laughs and cackles with passionate desire
And takes me over for it is so strong.
Despite my good intentions,
Greed has swallowed me.
It cuts through the sky
And spreads over the world.

Louise Rogers (10)
Old Vicarage School

Autumn

I see the leaves,
Green, yellow, gold and red,
So lovely to see them fall from the tree,
From the window by my bed.

The nights are getting darker
And the stars glisten through the night,
It is lovely to see the light from the window,
The glow is very bright.

I smell the horse chestnuts
That are cooking for me,
I quietly fall asleep
And I dream of a horse chestnut tree.

I lie by the fire,
Thinking sleepily,
About the beautiful autumn
And how lovely it can be.

Lydia Guest (10)
Old Vicarage School

Witch

She was bent and cold, like a tree in the woods with no leaves.
Her hair was burnt straw which had been set alight.
The feet were like curved leaves falling onto the winter's ground.
Her eyes were like coal glowing in the winter's night.
Her hands were sharp as eagle's claws.

Her clothes were all ragged like a scarecrow's clothes
Which had been left for twenty years.
Her hat was pointed like a sharp knife.

Louisa Azis (10)
Old Vicarage School

Autumn

Autumn's colours,
A riot of reds, oranges and yellows,
Like a warm fire when you come in from a cold day.

Autumn's sounds,
Birdsong and falling leaves,
So quiet and peaceful, like you're the only human left.

Autumn's tastes,
A warm, delicious blackberry pie,
You picked the berries and it's home-made by your mum.

Autumn's smells,
Warm soup and fresh berries,
Just right after a cold walk in the park.

Autumn's feelings,
Cold, refreshing and crisp,
Just like the day that it was first made.

Ellen O'Neill (9)
Old Vicarage School

My Mum

She is like a lily because she is always there smiling at you.
She is like a peacock's feathers because she has lots of
                                        different beauties in her.
She is like a clock because she is constant and is always there for you.
She is like a chilly, cloudless autumn day when all you see
                              are the gold leaves whirling like her hair.
She is like the colour yellow because she is the sun in the
                                 sky and always following me.
She is my mum.

Maggie Gray (10)
Old Vicarage School

The Rainy Day

Splash!
The rain falls to the earth,
The slippery puddles join together,
The rough moisture in the air feels so cold.
It feels as if your brothers are slapping you in the face.
As I walk through the street I tackle the rain,
As the wild wind tries to grab my umbrella.
The shower of rain makes the grass go wild
And the trees fly with the wind.
The leaves are being swept away,
To form a big swirl in the air.
The rain is drizzly now and there's a cool breeze in the air.
The small heads stick out of people's houses,
The puddles of water start to evaporate.
The rain is only spitting and children
Are coming out to play.

Shaima Mirza (10)
Old Vicarage School

The Jungle Playground

In the jungle there's a playground,
the best as best can be,
the monkey swings on the monkey bars
and the snake slithers with glee.

The elephant makes a great slide,
the leopard is bounding around,
he's trying to figure out the roundabout,
who should pull it? - The wild hound!

The see-saw's made by the crocodile,
rather a violent one though, too rough,
the lion has just finished the swings
and the snake's gone off in a huff.

At last the playground is finished,
all the jungle cheer,
for they have completed the animal task,
which was to build a playground here.

Rebecca Krol (10)
Old Vicarage School

Fire

A pile of sticks, the tiger sleeps but ready to pounce
If he needs to. The tiger wakes after his long nap,
Gets up and prowls his plain in the afternoon heat.
The fire is just beginning, flickering in the dark,
When out of the blue, another tiger, in his territory,
How dare he! Our friend must teach him to see
That this land is his.
The fire is beginning to get angry, flames circling, licking
All they can find and the tiger begins to fight.
He pounces on the newcomer, they grapple in their rage.
The flames are leaping, towering above everything around
And the tigers battle on, for hours on end,
Until our friend's enemy wavers and finally gives up.
The tiger proclaims his victory with a roar
That travels through his land.
The flames have ceased, it begins to drizzle,
It begins to rain.
Our tiger friend finds a cave and curls up,
Ready to sleep again.
He is not quite asleep, however,
For his fiery heart is still sparking.

Miranda Bowden-Doyle (10)
Old Vicarage School

I Saw . . .

I saw a tiger blaze and roar,
I saw a fire raise its paw.
I saw a stream ruffle and glow,
I saw a scrap of silk glide and flow.
I saw a butterfly shine and glitter in the sky,
I saw the stars flutter by.
I saw a snake, shrivelled and thin,
I saw the willow tree shedding its skin.
I saw the boy who saw all these things.

I saw an old tawny owl say goodnight,
I saw the man in the moon take flight.
I saw the sun sink in the caves,
I saw a turtle go under the waves.
I saw the green grass chuckle and sing,
I saw the little girl sway and swing.
I saw a thunderbolt tremble in fright,
I saw a field mouse raging with all its might.
I saw the lady who saw all these things.

Victoria James (10)
Old Vicarage School

Dogs

I went to the pound
To get a hound,

The keeper said, 'What do you want?
We've got the lot. We've got . . .

Mean dogs, lean dogs,
Hairy dogs, scary dogs,

Cool dogs, tall dogs,
Loud dogs, proud dogs,

Bony dogs, lonely dogs,
Skinny dogs, mini dogs,

Snappy dogs, happy dogs,
Wise dogs, prize dogs,

Lazy dogs, crazy dogs,
Fluffy dogs, scruffy dogs,

Bad dogs, mad dogs
And very, very sad dogs,

Waggy dogs, saggy dogs
And very, very baggy dogs.

So what do you want today?
Which dog do you want to take away?'

Ellie Williams (10)
Old Vicarage School

Anger

Anger is that trickle of blood
Running down your cheek
As hungry for a victim
As the crocodiles in a creek
When you come near it
It waits visible to some
When you get close enough
It jumps up and seizes you
Like a prowling cat
Anger is that flame
That destroyed many a house
It is an emotion that sometimes
Is hard to douse
It's that satanic wind
Uprooting and disrupting
Anything in its path
Anger is that spark inside
That when lit has to show
A freshly kindled fire
That will continually glow.

Shruti Sitaram (10)
Old Vicarage School

Bonfire Night

A hiss and a crackle, catching on the dry moss,
Leaves and twigs.
The smoke twisting upwards in a coil,
Disappearing into the black night
Like a soul from a dead body.
Darts of flame like slender figures
Reaching up as if to snare the stars.
Tongues of flame licking the sky
Like an excited child licking a lolly.
The bonfire blazes, twists and flails
Like a person in anger.
The smell of smoke is acrid and bitter
Like a person full of jealousy.
The flames leap, like mysterious spirits dancing.
Sparks fly, then disappear to nothing.
Then the fire begins to die down,
Like a weary person drifting to sleep.
Only the glowing embers, white ashes
And blackened and scorched grass
Are left after a hurricane of anger.

Catherine Neale (11)
Old Vicarage School

The Empty Bench

I sit alone on the bench by the pond,
Where Mary used to sing her song.
I walk by the river, no hand in mine,
When Mary was there we would be just fine.

In the playground only one swing swings,
In the playground, I make no rings.
In the park the Frisbee never returns,
Whenever this happens my heart always burns.

I'll never see Mary ever again,
No longer will we meet in our den.
No longer will I brush her hair,
No longer will we giggle on the stair.

Now it's time to end the rhyme,
But I don't think that I'll be fine.
She won't come back, never again,
I'll just have to find a new best friend.

Helena Westerman (10)
Old Vicarage School

My Sister

Identical to the colour grey, as teardrops are falling like rain,
Also, like the colour red, as her face darkens from its usual pale white,
The colour grows like an opening rose to a dark flaming red,
She's the same as the growing noise of the approaching storm.

The storm rages fiercely,
Her cries are like the howling wind,
She bangs the floor with her heels,
Just like the sound of hail on the window,
Like a lion roaring mad,
She shouts and rants at me,
The same as the thunderstorm,
With lightning crashing to the ground,
Like a rose with thorns covering it from top to bottom,
Whilst scratching at me, over and over.

Then it starts to quieten,
The gales of crying begin to pass away,
The flood of tears dries up like the passing rain,
The colour leaves her face and like the end of the storm,
She smiles - the sun comes out again!

Lucinda Barry (10)
Old Vicarage School

Rainy Day

Wellingtons and umbrellas,
Raincoats and hats,
Splish-splash in puddles,
Pouring down in torrents.
The hill becomes a stream,
The river is a swirling mass,
Pitter-patter goes the rain.
It's drenching the town.
The thunderous clouds,
Black as coal.
Splish-splash go my trainers,
My umbrella's turning inside out.
The birds are perched miserably,
Their feathers ruffled to keep them warm.
My hair looks like rats' tails sticking to my face.
The sky is clearing,
I'm soaked to the skin,
There's some bright blue sky and
A shining sun.

Lucy Cowen (10)
Old Vicarage School

Kennings - Dog!

Bone-taker
Tail-wagger
Lazy-sleeper
Paw-shaker
Lead-tugger
Noisy-barker
Face-licker
Sock-player
Fast-runner
Food-stealer
Lively-leaper
Floor-printer
Toy-fetcher
Plant-wrecker
High-jumper
Non-talker
Cat-catcher
Bark-woofer.

Lucy Iremonger (9)
Old Vicarage School

Laziness

The colour is a lovely milky brown
It tastes like rich milk chocolate
It smells of freshly cut grass
It looks like a shiny golden day
It sounds like a bird tweeting in the morning
It feels like I'm lying in the melting sun
And I feel like a sleeping, lazy, fat dog.

Ben Large (11)
Reigate St Mary's Preparatory & Choir School

Happiness

What colour is it?
It is a cheerful bright yellow.
What does it taste like?
It tastes like warm, melted marshmallows.
What does it smell like?
It smells like a steaming hot chocolate on a snowy winter's night.
What does it look like?
It looks like a beautiful meadow full of wild flowers
And bunnies with snow-capped mountains in the distance.
What does it sound like?
It sounds like my friends and I, laughing hysterically.
What does it feel like?
It feels like warm, soft fur against your cheek.

Thomas Williams (11)
Reigate St Mary's Preparatory & Choir School

Happiness

Happiness is the colour of bright gold.
Happiness tastes like strawberry ice cream with
                              delicious chocolate sprinkles.
Happiness smells like a bouquet of beautiful flowers.
Happiness looks like the biggest gold bar ever.
Happiness sounds like children happily laughing on the beach.
Happiness feels like melting chocolate dripping into your mouth.

Alexander Brumwell (10)
Reigate St Mary's Preparatory & Choir School

Anger

Anger is a blood-red mixed in a deep dark black,
It tastes like a shattered bottle falling down your throat,
It smells like a rotting bull carcass rotting all year,
It looks like a monster that a little kid made up,
It feels like water slowly dripping on your head for hours.

Jordan Carey (10)
Reigate St Mary's Preparatory & Choir School

Sadness

It's the colours black and grey for the darkness of this day.
It tastes of ash disappearing in my empty mouth.
It smells of smoke and fire as if I were in the middle of a
room of steam.
It looks like a rotting flower about to decay.
It sounds like no one can listen but I can't speak.
It feels like the darkness of sorrow is filling up inside me with
no other thought or feeling.

Elizabeth Boodhoo (10)
Reigate St Mary's Preparatory & Choir School

Happiness

Happiness is the brightest red like the flames of the sun,
It tastes like strawberry-flavoured ice cream refreshing my tongue,
It smells like vanilla and strawberry mixed together,
It looks like a soothing milkshake in the scorching sun,
It sounds like a bird singing through the fresh air,
It feels like a beach on a tropical island.

Aditya Gandhi (10)
Reigate St Mary's Preparatory & Choir School

Happiness

Happiness is a bright sunny yellow.
It feels like the juices on rough skin.
It has an aroma of lilies.
It tastes of the ripest mangoes on a hot summer's day.
It sounds like a jungle full of chirping birds.

Adam Vidler (11)
Reigate St Mary's Preparatory & Choir School

Happiness

Happiness is a bright fluorescent pink,
It tastes like warm, melted chocolate running down your throat.
It smells of roses in a meadow on a hot summer's day
And my favourite perfume.

Happiness looks like a great big smile on your rosy-red cheeks,
It sounds like a gentle river trickling through the rocks
On a green, grassy valley and laughter from a playground.
Happiness feels like warm and bubbly milk.

Hilary Stoughton (11)
Reigate St Mary's Preparatory & Choir School

Anger Poem

Anger is the colour of the deepest darkest black in Hell.
Anger tastes like hot, burning oil - incinerating your throat.
Anger smells like a hundred rotting, infested bodies.
Anger sounds like soldiers roaring into battle.
Anger looks like a black bomb about to explode - tick, tick, tick . . .
Anger feels like you want a sword in your hand to smash
                                        up everything in sight.

Euan Tilling (11)
Reigate St Mary's Preparatory & Choir School

Love Poem

Love is a flamingo-pink,
It tastes like sweet white chocolate,
It smells like 'Poeme' perfume wafting through the air,
Love looks like love hearts in an infant's eyes,
It sounds like nightingales in the morning, singing brightly,
It feels like soft, comfy cushions and lovely pink and
                                        yellow flowers around you.

Zach Sullivan (10)
Reigate St Mary's Preparatory & Choir School

Confusion

Confusion is a deep purple but changes its colour every time
you look away, in fact it doesn't know what colour it wants to be.

It tastes like bitter candyfloss fizzing on my tongue, with sour juice
dripping down my throat, changing its flavour whilst it goes down my
digestive system.

It smells like an unknown scent from afar flying up my left nostril and
coming out my right.

Confusion is like a million people, their words like arrows piercing my
heart, all trying to get my attention.

Confusion is a dark purple pit with unknown creatures with long
stretchy green antennas walking up people's throats and coming out
of their nostrils. Their eyes are like mystery, their noises are like
wonder.

Confusion feels like a surface made out of still living critters and when
you touch them they crawl up your arm, down your shirt and down your
trousers.

Luke Cattaneo (11)
Reigate St Mary's Preparatory & Choir School

Fear

What colour is it? Fear is a ghostly grey.
What does it taste like? It tastes like an old furry lollipop.
What does it smell like? Fear smells like old pond water.
What does it look like? It looks like a foggy landscape.
What does it sound like? Fear sounds like an old piece of chalk
                                  slowly pulling across a blackboard.
What does it feel like? It feels like you're being strangled.

Pascal Sedgwick (10)
Reigate St Mary's Preparatory & Choir School

Fear

What colour is fear? Fear is a dark, gloomy yellow.
What does fear taste like? Fear tastes of disgusting, off milk
letting off a disgusting smell.
What does fear smell like? Fear smells like old rotten vegetables.
What does fear look like? Fear looks like a long never-ending tunnel
that leads to nothingness.
What does fear sound like? Fear sounds like a continued whistling
in my mind.
What does fear feel like? Fear feels like I am shrinking into a
tiny small dot.

Tiarnan Cotter (11)
Reigate St Mary's Preparatory & Choir School

Happiness

Happiness is bright blue like the sky above.
It tastes like vanilla ice cream dripping off a cone
And smells like rich Terry's Chocolate Orange.
Happiness looks like a balloon floating up into the sky.
It sounds like Blur (Song 2)
And feels like walking on snow for the very first time.

George Hannigan (11)
Reigate St Mary's Preparatory & Choir School

Happiness

What colour is it? Happiness is a bright pink.
What does it taste like? It tastes like warm fudge.
What does it smell like? It smells like my mum's perfume.
What does it look like? It looks like a pink fluffy teddy bear.
What does it sound like? It sounds like children's laughter.
What does it feel like? It feels like squidgy cushions on a cosy sofa.

Benjamin Saward (10)
Reigate St Mary's Preparatory & Choir School

Happiness

Happiness is white because white is a mixture of every colour,
It looks like a bright rainbow glistening in the morning sun,
It smells like sweet flowers in the meadow,
It tastes like chocolate cake just baked and sitting on the window sill,
It sounds like rock 'n' roll playing in your back garden
And you are the only one who can hear it,
It feels like sleeping in a silk bed.

James O'Sullivan (10)
Reigate St Mary's Preparatory & Choir School

Worry

Worry is grey - a darkish grey
It tastes like dark black, hot coal
It smells like old stale cheese
It looks like a field of hazy smoke
It sounds like a thunderous, howling gale that won't stop
It feels like I am somewhere that no one else is around
And my future is uncertain.

Alexander Cloake (10)
Reigate St Mary's Preparatory & Choir School

Sadness

Sadness is a dark, gloomy, depressing blue,
It tastes like the morning dew,
It smells like a sweet flower upon a coffin of a loved one,
Sadness looks like a coffin in the back of a hearse,
It sounds like many a person weeping and sobbing a puddle
And it feels like tears running down your cheek.

Ryan Smith (11)
Reigate St Mary's Preparatory & Choir School

Happiness

Happiness is bright orange.
It tastes like warm, melted chocolate.
Happiness smells like my favourite perfume.
It looks like people smiling with joy.
Happiness sounds like laughter filling me with thoughts of paradise.
It feels like sunrays beating down on me.

Samantha Cloake (10)
Reigate St Mary's Preparatory & Choir School

Laziness

What colour is it? It is a dark, sludgy brown.
What does it taste like? The warm saliva dribbling onto your pillow.
What does it smell like? The hay when you're resting in a stable.
What does it look like? Lots of people slumbering.
What does it sound like? Annoying, loud snoring.
What does it feel like? Laziness feels like a soft pillow that won't let go.

Rufus Cuthbert (10)
Reigate St Mary's Preparatory & Choir School

Anger

What colour is it? Anger is the deepest darkest red from Hell.
What does it taste like? It tastes like raw, bloody meat on your tongue.
What does it smell like? It smells like acrid smoke gas
                                        flowing in the air.
What does it sound like? It sounds like a man dying on a fire.
What does it feel like? It feels like you want to punch
                                        and kick someone.

Sam Gregson (11)
Reigate St Mary's Preparatory & Choir School

Anger

Anger is a thundering torrent of flaming red.
Anger tastes like raw meat that has decayed over the years.
It smells like the black smoke from an active volcano
                              destroying your nose.
It looks like an angry, rampaging bull with death in his eyes.
Anger sounds like nails screeching down a blackboard
                              and burning your ears.
It feels like being thrown into a red-hot furnace and hearing innocent
                              souls screaming out in pain.

Oliver Horne (11)
Reigate St Mary's Preparatory & Choir School

Before The Trip To The Hospital

Portable TV
Comfort me,
Old teddy
Relieve me,
Mother's arms
Intense me,
Golden sun lead me to your window.
As the smiling nurses guide me to the hospital bed,
So may I dodge the elderlies' sticks in this terrible hospital,
As the smell of gas revolts me,
So may I not fear too much.
Terrible hospital find me,
Lead me to my mum.

Clare Fortune (9)
St Francis Catholic Primary School, Caterham

Before The Match

Chelsea ticket,
Come to me,
Glistening sun,
Guide me,
Wonderful sweet shop,
Draw me near,
Chelsea helping,
Show me
To my seat,
As the players walk
Onto the pitch,
So may I
Listen to the crowd,
Cheering on Chelsea,
As the players start
The game
So may I
Start to cheer with the crowd,
Frank Lampard hear me,
Football match let
Me have fun,
When the game is over
Chelsea have won.

Connor Cody (9)
St Francis Catholic Primary School, Caterham

Before Traffic

Speed cameras,
Miss me.
Traffic lights,
Turn green.
Car in front,
Go faster.
Let me get there soon.
Traffic jam,
Move along.
As the old lady crosses,
So may I
Avoid her.
As I whizz past
As the children
Play in the park,
So may I
Be first to finish the race.
Winning cup come to me,
Let me win the race.

Mary Fothergill (9)
St Francis Catholic Primary School, Caterham

Before The Sleep

Cosy bed,
Cuddle me.
Cosy pillow,
Warm me.
Cosy bed, cuddle me through the night.
When I fall into a deep sleep
I will feel the cooling breeze.
When I wake up, I will see the light of the day.
Morning is nigh!

Mark Cuthbert (8)
St Francis Catholic Primary School, Caterham

Before The Football Match

Once I wake up,
I get excited,
I can't help it,
So please calm me.
Once I get up,
Stop me from bursting,
Help me
Prepare for my match.
Once I have my breakfast,
Convince me
To do my teeth,
Quickly!
Once I'm in the car,
Hear me
As I shuffle about
In the moving car.
Once I'm on the pitch,
I'm nervous,
But excited,
Help me, please!

David Pullinger (9)
St Francis Catholic Primary School, Caterham

Before Midnight

Howling wolves touch me, swaying trees feel me.
Dancing moon sparkle through the night.
So you can shine above the stars in the night sky.
So may I dance alone in the dark night sky
And let the stars shine up over the moon.

Lani Hall (9)
St Francis Catholic Primary School, Caterham

Before I Go To Bed

Yummy tea,
Fill me,
Creaky stairs,
Scare me,
Drink of water,
Calm me,
Electric toothbrush,
Fill my mouth with bubbles,
As the rain pours
Down outside,
So may I
Change into my PJs
And out of my slippers,
As I put my hair up,
So may I jump onto my bed,
In my quilt,
I am scared of the nightmares all around,
Help me teddy,
Help me please,
Help me to my sleep.

Elizabeth Lawless (9)
St Francis Catholic Primary School, Caterham

How

Bathing in a swimming pool
That is how girls keep cool.
Scaring girls, making them scream
That is how boys are made so mean.
Chasing boys is what girls like best
That is how they get no rest.
Playing with guns, bows and arrows
That is how boys scare the sparrows.
Some are good and some are bad.
Some are and some are not.
I give up, my brain is getting hot!

Cherise Pullin (8)
St Francis Catholic Primary School, Caterham

Before The Death

Big knife
Scare me,
Wet eyes
Shake me,
Dry hanky
Calm me,
Almighty God
Protect my
Family every day.
As the people around me
Cry with anger,
So may I not be sad
For my whole lifetime.
As the priest talks about
That special person,
So may I not sob too much.
Lovely angels, smile at me,
Bad devils, leave me,
Please look after my dad.

Rocio Crispin (8)
St Francis Catholic Primary School, Caterham

Before The Shop

Smiling staff
Calm me,
Fresh vegetables
Heal me,
Heated chicken
Heat me,
Guiding signs
Lead me to the sections.

When we go to the counter,
We pay our daily food
And off we go.

Martin Rawlings (8)
St Francis Catholic Primary School, Caterham

Before The Car Trip

Flowing water
Wash away
Down my mouth.
'Go to the toilet!'
My mum shouts.
I put the dog in
The car, *woof!*
In the car we get,
Which way? That way!
Off we go!
The car, as fast as a cheetah.
'Wind the window down!'
'It's cold,
Wind the window up!'
'Sh! He's sleeping!'
'Stop peeping!'
Woof, woof!
'Be quiet, doggy.'
'Waa, waa,' my sister shouts.
'Stop here, we need to let
The dog out!'
'Help me out!'

Emily Pemberton (8)
St Francis Catholic Primary School, Caterham

Before The Hunt Through The Woods

Cold wind
Hear me,
Swaying trees
Help me,
Windy breeze
Calm me,
Cloudy sky
Light my way home.
As the animals
Protect the forest,
As the dog
Sniffs his way,
So may I be first through the Hunt.
Noisy forest
Hear me,
Chilling breeze
Still my body,
Teasing monkey smile with me,
Lead me to my home.

Andre Anastasi (9)
St Francis Catholic Primary School, Caterham

The Race To School

Rushing people
Wait for me,
Talking teachers
Listen to me,
Cooling breeze
Calm me,
Dark path
Light my way to school.
As the people go hurrying by,
So may I
Go as fast as them.
As they get faster and faster,
So may I
Be faster as well.
St Francis School reward me,
Happy helpers cheer for me,
Help me to win the race.

Sally Stevens (8)
St Francis Catholic Primary School, Caterham

Before Gymnastics Class

Mum and Dad
Watch me,
Fittest teachers
Call me,
Strong muscles
Help me to last this class.
As I jump onto the box,
The teacher says, 'Good!'
So may I
Be as good as them,
When I am older.
As I watch the trampoline class
Go up and down,
So may I
Be first to get a badge.
Mum and Dad watch me,
Fittest teachers call me,
Help me to last this class.

Heather Lafferty (8)
St Francis Catholic Primary School, Caterham

Who Flushed My Great Granny Down The Toilet?

Who flushed my great granny down the toilet?
She was my favourite granny
And all she left me was her hairnet.

She gave me banana milkshake,
She gave me sweets,
I was too late for her sake
And now she is swimming in the
Sewer under the streets.

Now a month has passed
And I really miss her.
Well, time goes fast
I wonder what she is doing in the sewer
So don't you flush
Your granny down
The toilet
Or else.

Kerry Brown (9)
St Francis Catholic Primary School, Caterham

Before Pop Music

Rock music
Thrill me,
Play guitars
Tempt me,
Be unbearable,
Please me,
Be raging,
Make my
Eardrums burst,
As the drums *bang!*
So may I
Be in the band like you,
As you are really noisy,
So may I
Be unbearable like you,
When I'm older
I want to be in the band
And after I'll be playing in the sand.

Ryan Norman (8)
St Francis Catholic Primary School, Caterham

Shane

There once was a boy called Shane
Who lived tied up in chains
He tried to get out
But without a doubt
He ended up insane!

Louis Brooker (10)
St Paul's CE Primary School, Addlestone

What Makes A Good Friend?

Sprinkle a hint of friendship around the classroom,
Spray a bit of laughter in the class,
Throw a load of happiness around all your friends,
Put the arguments in boiling water until they dissolve.
Scatter some kindness around the room,
Throw a handful of helpfulness around your friends,
Shower your friends with love,
Powder some goodness around your friendship
And it will make it last forever.
Spread some enjoyment,
Have fun and be merry,
Make new friends and fill up with joy.
Use happy thoughts when missing your friends.
Fill you and your friends with delightfulness,
Make sure you always sort out your problems
To make it last and you will find the perfect friend in the end.

Victoria Osborne (7)
St Paul's CE Primary School, Addlestone

Tsunami

On that warm and sunny day
It was lovely and calm
No one could know of the harm!

It took out lives,
Laid them flat.
Separated families,
Split them apart!

Now we pray for those people,
Hope they're living.

Jack Ward (7)
St Paul's CE Primary School, Addlestone

Prayer For Victims Of The Tsunami

Dear God,
Something happened far away from here,
The whole world had a little tear,
How could it be?
I just don't understand
How it destroyed all these lands.
Please make them safe,
And hold them close to you,
Tell them we think about them too.
Bless St Paul's because we care
And help us teach the world to share.

Amen.

Emily Bradly (6)
St Paul's CE Primary School, Addlestone

We Remember The Tsunami

People were happy playing,
Homes were nice and neat.
When a gigantic tidal wave
Came and swept you off your feet.
People ran for help,
Running with pets like a mouse.
Almost everything washed away,
All that was left was a fallen house.
We think of the people
Who have no family.
It would be terrible
To happen to me.

Jemma Waldock (7)
St Paul's CE Primary School, Addlestone

The Candy Man

The candy man came to our house last night
He took every toy, every sweet in sight
He took down the shelves, the frames and the light
And, oh my gosh, he gave me a fright.

He ran down the street with my brother's sheet
And on the way he did say, for all the damage he would pay
So he went home to his candy cone
And he called me the next day on the phone

'I'm sorry, I'm sorry for all the things I've done
Please let me have another cream bun
Please can I see you another time again?
I even might let you have another cream hen!'

Elyse Kennedy (9)
St Paul's CE Primary School, Addlestone

The Bogeyman

A bogeyman came to my town last night,
He stole every child that was in sight,
He went through the houses,
He went through the street,
He saw little Peter, dressed all neat.

He jumped out at Peter and gave him a fright,
Poor little Peter ran all through the night,
He went to his mum and then his dad,
Oh my gosh, Peter he did get mad.
He shouted to the heavens above,
Suddenly, the bogeyman let go of a dove.
The dove meant peace,
All the bogeyman wanted was his little niece.

Zoë Coombs (10)
St Paul's CE Primary School, Addlestone

What Is Autumn?

Autumn is conkers,
swinging round on strings.
Sights of leaves falling
gracefully off the trees.
Animals are squirrels
stacking acorns for the winter.
Autumn is hedgehogs
crawling round gardens.
That's what autumn is!

Anais Longeville (10)
St Paul's CE Primary School, Addlestone

Monkey Dance

There is a monkey in me,
He never hides,
He's always out playing,
He has dark eyes of black, like coal
And he has brown and white fur,
Like red heeled knee socks.
He oohs and aahs like an audience,
He lives in the vines of my brain
And swings like a coin on a silver string.
He makes me do
The monkey dance
Oh! Oh! Oh! - Ah, Ah!
The monkey dance
Oh! Oh! Oh! - Ah, Ah!
The monkey dance!

Justin Hernandez (11)
TASIS

There Is A Cat In Me

In me there is a cat,
just as mighty as a lion.

It helps me control my anger
and let it out when the right time comes.

That cat in me has reflexes as good as any,
though on my own
I don't always land on my feet.

That cat in me is curious,
with nothing to feed her need to explore.

In me there is a cat,
just as mighty as a lion.

Anneliese Rinaldi (10)
TASIS

Mouse Man

There is a mouse in me
With a clever mind
Who likes to take a dollar
Or two when not in view
I run, walk, talk when I wish to
I'm timid, but will take a risk
Or even try something new
I move slowly but can accomplish
A very great speed too
A little creature like me has a great voice
And a hidden power of strength
I am a true mouse man!

Liam Gaughan (10)
TASIS

Zebra Unleashed

There is a zebra in me,
Black and white silky stripe,
That no other has.
Galloping on the wind,
It's wild and independent.
It lives in my heart, waiting to be freed.
As I step out the door and live on my own,
It will break free
And be as happy as me.
But it won't stay in my heart for long,
By then it will be just a happy memory and song.

Sofia Santacaterina (10)
TASIS

Snake

There is a snake in me
With scales as green as emeralds,
It hisses like a lizard in a tree,
It creeps like a lion catching its prey,
It has eyes like opals,
It lives in my heart and makes me happy,
I wish I was that snake.

Christopher Aguais (10)
TASIS

Inside The Ocean

Inside the ocean
is life beyond life
it's a mystery to be solved
amazing things yet to be found
the ocean is a miracle
even better than the ground.

Inside the ocean is a surface
with no end
with no control
creating disasters
or creating fun
nothing will stop the ocean.

Emma Grant (10)
TASIS

Backpacks

Books of all sizes, shapes and subjects,
Activities and homework,
Comfortable straps on my back,
Kangaroos have pockets just like my backpack.
Pencils, pens, markers, crayons,
Pencil sharpeners and erasers,
Arts and crafts I make at school,
Cameras to take on field trips,
To savour the memories,
Knowledge of all the books in the bag.

David Dover (11)
TASIS

Animal In Me

There is a dog in me
With fur like
My furry coat
It wiggles when I play
It lives in my heart
And makes me breathe
When I play, it comes out of my heart
And plays with me
It makes me feel like
Playing all day
I wish he would come out
More than twice a day.

Sarah Trudelle (11)
TASIS

There's A Hamster In Me

There is a hamster in me
With fur like silk
And paws so quick
It squeaks like hinges
On a broken door
It wiggles like a worm
It lives in my liver
And makes me shiver
I wish it would come out
And let me keep it as a pet.

Alex Clark (10)
TASIS

Inside Your Parents

Inside your parents
is a photo album
of your childhood,
changing as time passes.
Inside is wisdom from the past,
advice waiting to be said,
knowledge as well.
Inside is fun, madness and patience,
stories and faces.
There is anger and love
and prayers for your safety,
forgiveness in times you've done wrong.
Inside your parents,
deeper down,
is love for you that no one can stop.
Your eyes cannot see all that is there.
There inside your parents
unseen and unknown.

Hannah Lowry (10)
TASIS

Chihuahua

There is a Chihuahua in me,
With fur as soft as a feather.
It goes *woof, woof* when it's happy
By wagging its tail.
It goes around like an explorer,
Trying to find a hot dog to eat.

It wiggles like a worm
And runs like a galloping horse.
It lives in my brain like donkeys do too
And all I want is to have a buddy like it.

Sofia Leiva (10)
TASIS

Inside A Mini Ipod

Inside a mini ipod
Is more than you think
Comes in many different colours
And many voices and thoughts
About people of fame and fortune

Listening to these voices
You may learn a lot more than you think
Than just someone called a star
That you dream you will be
Mini ipods
Are more than just a harmony.

Annie Gaughan (10)
TASIS

Super Hamster

There is a hamster in me,
To run fast and play in paper,
They are small and timid,
They like to nibble
And they have fur,
They're friendly
Like a family.

Simon Bedard (11)
TASIS

Inside A Book

Inside a book
there are many different things,
just waiting to be found.
Apart from the words,
lines and pictures,
there are feelings,
love, just waiting to be let out.
They are amazing things,
although they don't look it.
But if you look deeper inside,
past all the words, lines and pictures,
you'll see what a book is all about.
The author takes a lot of care
to make a book for you.
If you look, listen and watch,
you might see what his or her life is like.
So next time you read a book,
have a look and see
what the author's words are saying
and maybe you'll find out
what the book is about.

Anouka Pedley-Egan (10)
TASIS

The Lonely Little Flower

Dancing in the rain, swaying in the breeze,
Lonely little flower, living amongst the trees.

Petals facing upward, turned toward the sky,
So all the little children will look when they pass by.

They admire all your beauty, until winter comes,
When you will fall to the ground and your petals will turn numb.

Emily Churchill (11)
TASIS

A Memory

I remember
The beautiful meadow,
The sweet smell of the flowers.

I remember
The bluebells,
As blue as the ocean.

I remember
The daffodils,
As yellow as the sun.

I remember
The orchid
As pink as a pig.

There was a
Light breeze.

The sun shone
More brightly
Than I've ever
Seen before.

Chloe Ridgway-Smith (10)
The Hawthorns School

What Is Rain?

Rain is the tears shed from a giant.
Rain is a leak from a great tap.
Rain is the sky falling down.
Rain is a river in the sky that has burst its banks.
Rain is the spray from a waterfall.
Rain is the dribble from a teething baby.
Rain is not what you think.

Alexander McNeil (9)
The Hawthorns School

Winter

I am the one who ices up your windows,
I am the one who fogs up your car windows,
On a cold morning, I am the one who lines the grass with frost,
I am the one who gives you snow,
I am *winter.*

I am the one whom you hear whispering through the air,
I am the one whom you hear when the ice cracks,
I am the one you hear when the wind is banging against the window,
I am *winter.*

I am the one you taste when the cold ice touches your tongue,
I am the one whom you taste when the snow gently falls onto your lip,
I am *winter.*

Libby Russell-Watts (10)
The Hawthorns School

Old House

I have creaky floorboards
That are lonely and broken,
My rusty gate, damp and dusty,
That was bright as gold,
My cellar dark and gloomy,
That had a party so many times,
My attic, damp and forgotten,
That had toys,
My garden is dark and sad,
That was once happy and joyful,
But my time here is close to go,
A shopping mall and market is now,
Goodbye, I stand no more.

Tom Prosser (10)
The Hawthorns School

The General

What does he hear?
Babies screaming,
People crying,
Bombs exploding, killing the enemy,
The swords slashing!

What does he feel?
He feels the slimy blood,
He feels the sharp sword,
He feels the sandy grass,
He feels the cold air, as he rides faster and faster on his horse.

What does he dream of?
He dreams of living, of winning, of happiness,
To see his family,
To go home safe and sound.

Tayler Phelps (10)
The Hawthorns School

Summer

I am the one who makes the flowers bloom red and orange,
I am the one who causes the sun to shine,
I am the one that makes the sea cool
And I am the one after spring.

I am the one that tells the bees to buzz,
I am the one who gives you beautiful weather,
I am the warming finger pointing at you,
I am the one before autumn.

I am the one who makes the clear skies,
I am the one who makes the grass green,
I am the one and only summer,
I am the one who now has to go.

Pascale Davies (10)
The Hawthorns School

The Enchanted Garden

I can see . . .

Silky skirts swaying as fairies dance
And they glide across the pond with fishes too
And luminous lights
Around the edge.

I can smell . . .

The flowers in the air
And the fresh-smelling honey
From the bees.

I can hear . . .

The crickets clicking,
The birds cheeping
And the frogs croaking,
The grass, sprouting up to the sky.

Calm and peaceful,
In the enchanted garden.

Jenny Wijsmuller (11)
The Hawthorns School

What Is The Moon?

The moon is a dinosaur egg in its black nest of burnt
                                        twigs and leaves.
It is a white thumb print on a black piece of paper.
It is a silver penny dropped down a drain in Heaven by the gods.
It is a round sparkling diamond in the rock it grew in.
It is a white pizza spinning round and round on its black plate of ash.
It is a white football kicked high in the air from a stadium far away.
It is a little round stone thrown high in the air from its soft
                                        bed of leaves.

Luke Andrews (10)
The Hawthorns School

A Garden Grows With Roses

A garden grows with roses as
English grows with words.

Words that are free as birds,
Words that are crumpled in herds.

Words that float around in my mind,
Words with explanations I cannot find.

Words that explain my utter desire,
Words that make me really inspired.

Words that drag me into a world of sadness,
Words that fill me with the guilt of badness.

Words that force me to feel really mean,
Words make you not want to be seen.

Emily Beater (9)
The Hawthorns School

A Monster's Favourite Thing To Eat

Slugs, worms, beetles' meat
Ladybugs' blood and gorillas' feet
Sizzling earwigs get stuck in his teeth
Hide under his tongue, right underneath
He crunches and gobbles, slurps and snorts
He's never polite with the food that he's caught
Warthogs' hooves and horses' hair
Try eating that, if you dare!
This monster is someone you wouldn't want to meet
As his breath must smell as bad as my feet!

Emily Lock (9)
The Hawthorns School

Safe

I ran away from home this year,
From gypsy boots and fists I fear.

Someone found me, I don't know how,
I'm safely in a kennel now.

I know I'm safe but I'm still wary
And still find big boots very scary.

Some dogs here are just 'short stay',
Their families are on holiday.

But I am here and all alone,
Until I find my perfect home.

Lots of people have been to see,
But so far, no one's chosen me.

I hope a family take me home,
So I'll have a place to call my own.

Lucy Blackwell (10)
The Hawthorns School

Gala

At last my time has come,
To do what has to be done.

A shiver runs down my spine,
As I step onto the blocks for the last time.

A beep fills my ears,
As I face my fears.

As I push off the blocks,
My legs feel like rock.

It all depends on me now,
Whether I win or not.

Jessica Pritchard (10)
The Hawthorns School

The Shadow Of The Black Knight

The shadow of the great black knight,
Galloping through the forests and woods,
In a speed which is hard to catch,
For his honour and victory.

The glittering streams get parted,
As his shadow carries on,
Through the caves of trolls and beasts,
For his honour and victory.

His gleaming armour shines,
Standing out in lightning storms,
The shield showing the courage inside,
For his honour and victory.

Slaying dragons as he goes,
Rescuing pretty damsels,
Returning back to the kingdom,
For his honour and victory.

James Burrows (10)
The Hawthorns School

My Sporty Family

Dad is the best footballer in the world!
He plays like Ronaldhinio,
Mum swims like a bottle-nosed dolphin,
Sister plays hockey like a pro,
Grandad ice-skates like Robin Cousins!
Nana does archery like Robin Hood,
Granny can juggle like a clown
And I can just do everything!

Tom Allen (10)
The Hawthorns School

The Elephant's Day

In his mud bath the elephant wallows,
His vast ears flapping lazily as he tries to keep cool,
He sinks down, his colossal legs collapsing under his great weight,
His scrawny tail floats out behind him like a piece of string.
With a resounding trumpet he clumsily heaves himself out of the
squelchy mud,
Casually he plods over to the nearest tree,
Enormous head swaying, he fells the unfortunate sapling,
Like a snake his trunk curls around the juicy leaves
And he devours them hungrily,
Replete, he settles down to a pleasant afternoon slumber,
The mud from his bath slowly drying in the hot African sun.

Kitty Tittle (10)
The Hawthorns School

The Scrapyard

The scrapyard is a place never visited by most humans,
But the ones that do go, they find all sorts of things, big or small,
The find engines, working or otherwise,
They find cogs, some rusty, some not,
They find tyres, some flat, some not,
They find hoses, some leaky, some not,
They find all varieties of cars, some new, some old,
The Earth is like a giant scrapyard,
People forever finding things, making things
And then using the parts for other contraptions
Of great beauty and wonder.

Aled Williams (9)
The Hawthorns School

The Dolphin

This creature it leaps,
It leaps gracefully,
It leaps, it leaps,
It leaps out of the sea.

The sun how it shines,
It shines, it shines,
On the beautiful sea,
Turquoise and lime.

When under the water,
It whirls, it whirls,
When under the water,
In circles, it twirls.

This creature, this creature,
To whom I must give praise,
When fighting the sharks,
My life it did save!

So this time when the dolphin
Leapt out of the sea,
On its smooth, streamline back,
It was carrying me!

Grace Oxenham (10)
The Hawthorns School

Coral Reef Poem

There I am swimming in the clear blue, clear blue, clear blue,
I can see some beautiful things, beautiful things, in the clear blue.
I can see a big thin tail upon its back, what is that?
I feel some stones and some sand on my hand.
Argh! What is that? Something is trying to drag me somewhere.
What is happening?
I smell blood and my knee is hurting so much.
I wish I didn't do that dive.
Now I'm here,
What happened?

Rebecca Fagan (10)
The Hawthorns School

When The Wave Came

When the wave came,
Total destruction took hold.
Lives were snuffed like a candle without air.

When the wave came,
My family went.
I don't know where.

When the wave came,
My town was destroyed.
My life blown apart.

When the wave came,
The landscape was cleaned.
Cleaned of life.

When the wave came,
The light vanished from the world
Leaving only blackness.

When the wave came,
My mind was scarred.
I cannot forget.

When the wave came,
The death toll amazed.
Help came, not to me.

When the wave came,
I found my mother
Lying with lifeless eyes.

When the wave came,
I found my father also
Lying, unmoving.

When the wave came,
I heard people's dying shouts.
They haunt me.

But when the wave came, I lived.

Lydia Bass (10)
The Hawthorns School

My Day At School

Bring, bring, there goes my alarm,
'It's time to get up my dear!'

Crunch, crunch, my buttery toast,
It's already gone, oh dear!

Beep, beep, there goes her horn,
It's Sarah, I'm late I fear!

Screech, screech, here's the drop-off zone,
Hooray, hooray, we're here!

Pant, pant, I'm out of breath,
It's registration, *I'm here!*

Natter, natter, now settle down,
It's lessons, oh great, oh dear!

Giggle, giggle, let's go and play,
Let's play when no one is near!

Gobble, gobble, it's lunchtime now,
Don't talk; a teacher is near!

Woo, woo, that's the whistle again,
It's lessons, just so typical here!

Hooray, hooray, we're going home,
Everyone starts to cheer!

Squish, squish, I'm making tea,
Dad is drinking beer!

Goodnight, goodnight, my little one,
Sleep well, I won't let the bedbugs near!

Emily Hocken (9)
The Hawthorns School

Short Celebrations

A majestic soldier,
Proud and tall,
Looking out of a cold, frosty window,
White, cotton snowflakes,
Falling from the dark sky.

Celebrations have finally arrived,
Time of goodwill, of giving,
To be happy and joyful.

Christmas Eve is here!

Boxes being opened,
One by one,
Baubles all shapes and sizes,
Glitter and shine.

Carefully and gently,
Drawing nearer and nearer,
Baubles being hung,
On my prickly branches.

Oh, how nice it feels,
To show off my branches,
Covered in bright tinsel.

A month has passed, still I stand,
Until one day, I am destroyed.

Boxes closed, one by one,
With baubles wrapped up,
Ready to begin again.

Snowflakes stop falling, the sun starts to shine,
The first sign of spring, sprouting in the ground.

But I do not stand any longer,
Prickly dead leaves, bare branches,
Make me look older and older.

Charlotte Hart (9)
The Hawthorns School

My Little Brother

On the 3rd February 2003,
Out popped my little brother, Bub,
By golly he really changed my life
And life as I knew it, had transformed.

Clinging to Mummy like a limpet,
I couldn't get a look in, I felt a bit left out,
Like an unwanted playmate in the playground.

Broken sleep, my little brother wailing in the night,
Like a forlorn bird, waiting impatiently in its nest for food.

His first year passed by quickly, as if time was flying by,
Crawling, then walking, then talking,
Suddenly my little brother seemed more fun.

Splashing puddles,
Like the plastic ducks he plays with in the bath.
Bouncing on the trampoline,
Like Tigger in Winnie the Pooh.

Dancing to my favourite CDs,
A mini Britney or Justin Timberlake,
Smearing on my make-up, lips as pink as his cheeks.

Now the terrible twos,
Stomping like an elephant if he doesn't get his way.
Screaming, throwing, yelling and ranting
Every single day.

It's not all that bad though, he's also very cute,
Kisses and cuddles, giggles and laughter.
Bringing light to my life and happiness to my heart.
Though he can be irritating,
In a cheeky sort of way,
To me he is a star,
My adorable little brother, Bub!

Laura Day (10)
The Hawthorns School

Wild Horses And Me

Wild horses fling their heads up high
I think they are going to touch the sky
Their coats are gleaming, glossy and bright
Their eyes sparkling in the sunlight
These horses are so strong and fast
If you blink you wouldn't know they've passed
They live in the wild with the birds and the trees
Trotting about in the blanket of leaves
Are they lonely or do they like to be free?
Maybe they want to spend some time with me
I watch them galloping and listen to the sound
Of hundreds of hooves as they hit the ground
Their tails are swaying in the misty air
Like carousel horses at a funfair
I wish I could watch them all day and all night
They really are an amazing sight
Wild horses fling their heads up high
They really are going to touch the sky.

Ellie Jackman (10)
The Hawthorns School

Sweetie Land

A land where trees are liquorice,
The trunks are covered with Turkish Delight.
Houses built from Smarties and candy sticks,
Decorated with fairy cakes.
Would you like to grow up here?
Edible things are always near.
When it rains, raindrops are sugar grains,
If you're sure you want to live out here,
Remember to bring your toothbrush! - Cheers.

Jonathan Chan (9)
The Hawthorns School

Gold

The sun is shining bright and hot,
The track is glistening in the blazing heat.
Tying my laces and stretching slowly,
The butterflies fluttering as I breathe in and out,
I bend and wait,
Not a sound, only the thumping of my heart.
Bang!

The crowd shout and scream,
I explode from the blocks as I stride out with pride,
My arms pushing and pulling and my legs pumping hard.
I feel others all around me catching up fast,
Searching for the line,
I am one step away,
I close my eyes with nerves as I reach the finish.
Gold!

Sam Grayston (9)
The Hawthorns School

Snow

S now silently fell from the dark sky,
N ot a sound was heard from a mouse or bird.
O ver the hills a blanket of bright wintry white snow.
W alking through the snow is a red-breasted robin.
F alling from the cloudy sky is a drop of life.
L anding late is a merry family of robins.
A mouse sheltered under a bush,
K eeping a watchful eye.
E vergreens showered in white snowy powder.
S ilent snowflakes softly lay.

Kathryn Dodds (9)
The Hawthorns School

Paradise Lost

Azure blue sky in paradise
Ocean as blue as the sky above in paradise
With the sun's warm rays giving life to paradise
Golden sand, happy people, children playing in
The gentle ocean waves in paradise
All the people from around the globe have come
To enjoy themselves in paradise
Laughter and birdsong and the music of the ocean
Waves, all playing in paradise
Gentle breeze whispering softly in the palm trees
And teasing the ocean waves
No, not a dream, this is paradise
All the world loves this paradise where the ocean
Is warm and teeming with life and where
The ocean invites you to swim and play
Where the ocean is gentle and good and alive
Azure blue sky in paradise
Ocean flowing further and further away from paradise
With the sun's warm rays giving life to paradise
Golden sand and all the people from around
The globe looking at the ocean flowing
Away from paradise
No more laughter, no more joy, just an almighty
Terrifying roar
A wall of water as high as a house
The ocean is drowning everyone in paradise
No, not a dream, this is paradise lost
All the world loves this paradise and all
The people from around the globe are uniting
In helping this place on Earth which is paradise.

Isabella Fernandes (10)
The Hawthorns School

What Is Sport?

What is rugby?
A bundle of muddy men in a pile.

What is squash?
Trainers squeaking, ball echoing, players sweating.

What is netball?
Dodging girls, strong passes, the goal shooter concentrating.

What is unihoc?
Clashing sticks, swift passes, skilful goals.

What is rounders?
Speedy runners, accurate throws, hot sunny days.

What is ballet?
Bright coloured costumes, strong gliding ballerinas, loud music from
the orchestra.

What is football?
Slippery, brown mud, enthusiastic spectators, headers scored from
corners.

What is swimming?
Flying butterfly, starter's whistle, diving like a bullet.

What is wrestling?
Sumo strength, beefy and powerful, referee counting 1 . . . 2 . . . 3.

What is sport?
Something *everyone* can have fun at.

Charlotte Dialdas (8)
The Hawthorns School

My Football Match

Come on Chelsea, come on Chelsea,
That's a bad tackle
'Send him off, Ref!'
Come on Chelsea, come on Chelsea,
Yes, a goal!
Half-time,
Time to get a snack,
Second half,
Come on Chelsea, come on Chelsea,
Yes, a goal!
That's a bad tackle,
Oh no! They've scored.
Come on Chelsea, come on Chelsea.
'Send him off, Ref!'
Come on Chelsea, come on Chelsea,
'That's not a foul, Ref.'
Oh no! They've scored.
Come on Chelsea, come on Chelsea,
Yes, a goal!
'That's a penalty, Ref!'
He steps up to take it and *whack,*
It's in the back of the net,
We've won! We've won!
Final score, 4-2 to Chelsea.

Thomas Fice (9)
The Hawthorns School

The Witches' Spell

Thrice the eye of a toad has shot out
A slimy worm is in doubt
The eagle dives - 'tis time, 'tis time
In goes a lizard's eye, full of slime

Frothing full, furious and fast
Drink the potion while it lasts!

Pigs' guts with loads of blood
Frogs' guts rolled in lots of mud
Wrinkled fingers, bloody and burned
Now 'tis time for lessons learned

Frothing full, furious and fast
Drink the potion while it lasts!

The hairy tail of a flea-infested rat
And the nose hairs of a cat
Add a seething mass of hair
Now's the time you cannot bear

Frothing full, furious and fast
Drink the potion while it lasts!

James Turner (10)
The Hawthorns School

A Bumblebee

I can see a bumblebee
Flying high in the sky
Making honey
To make some money
If they're frightened
They will sting
Something, anything, even string
Bumblebees feed on nectar and pollen
So they might go and land on something foreign.

James Miller (8)
The Hawthorns School

The Monkey

A monkey is a shy creature, it eats bananas,
Is brown, is funny,
Swings through the trees, is small
And I could afford one
With my mum's money!

If I had a monkey, it would be so much fun,
It would help me climb trees
And we could lie in the sun.

We could be best friends,
We could play football and computer games
And hopefully the monkey would not
Call me nasty names!

Actually, the more I think, I have a monkey of my own,
She is small and funny and plays with me,
She is my sister called Georgina,
Is she my best friend? - Well, maybe!

Jim Salmon (8)
The Hawthorns School

Brilliant Cornwall

The wind was howling round the bay,
The gulls were screeching - what did they say?
I heard a noise, was it a band?
No, just children playing in the sand.

Out at sea - the surfers so brave,
Waiting for that humungous wave,
Some caught the waves and then did fly,
I looked and hoped they would not die.

The boat in the estuary hoisted its sail,
Sitting and waiting for a giant gale,
People in Padstow eating ice cream
And then I woke up - it was all just a dream!

Henry Harrod (10)
The Hawthorns School

My Bedroom

My bedroom is an amazing place,
With all different coloured walls,
It's got a vast amount of space
And a lot of disco balls!
My bedroom has a plasma screen
And every DVD,
You may not fancy it yourself,
But it's paradise for me.

My bedroom's an exotic place,
Where I can always dream,
But some say that it's horrible,
Because it's not that clean.

I like to put up photographs
And all that sort of stuff,
There is just one thing wrong with it,
There's simply not enough!

I've got the latest Yamaha
And a flat screen Dell,
I never want to leave my room,
Because everywhere else is hell!

Oliver Whippey (10)
The Hawthorns School

Wipe Out!

Running on the warm sand, ahead of me the cold waves.
Out of breath, my heart is pounding, faster and faster and faster!
I grab my board and jump in, the freezing water splashes over me.
The wind is pushing me backwards as I wade out further and further.
'I think I see the big one! It's over there!' I shout.
I lie on my board waiting till it crashes over me.
Smash, tumble! The wave suddenly spins me around with its power.
My dad worries that I'm not OK, until I pop out and yell with a grin,
'Wipe out!'

William Guise (7)
The Hawthorns School

Wild Horses

Across the deep green moor under the starlit sky
Runs the grey mare,
Her head is held high,
Her tail streams behind her,
She makes no sound as her hooves touch the ground.
Her foal comes to join her,
His coat gleams in the twilight,
They dance in the moonlight and canter up the hill.
A black stallion meets them and joins in the dance,
He rears up and whinnies into the night.

Dawn has approached and the mare has gone,
The foal is not there for he has left with the mare.
The magic hour has been and gone,
The stallion looks up at the starlit night,
He is proud of his foal
Who looks down at him now,
A prince of the sky.

Alexandra Moyle (9)
The Hawthorns School

The Leaf

The leaf flourishes out of the branches of the oak . . .
The leaf flutters through the air and through the smoke . . .
The leaf falls to the ground and sinks in the mud . . .
The leaf fails to stay alive, it is crushed by a rugby stud . . .
The leaf falls into the dark never to be awoke . . .
The leaf flip-flops through the thick, billowing smoke . . . to death!

Callum McLaren (10)
The Hawthorns School

My Cats

We have two cats who are very dotty,
They're a breed of cats called Silver Spotty.
They're very clever, they're very funny,
One's called Tiger, one's called Honey.

At night they're really good,
Up to the point I give them food.
After that they run about the house,
I suppose they're looking for a spider or a mouse.

Honey often curls upon my bed
And I reach down and rub her head.
As I stroke my cat's fur,
She looks content and then starts to purr.

When prowling out late at night,
The neighbour's cat they often fight.
But whilst they often like to roam,
They're at their happiest when they come home.

Molly Abraham (8)
The Hawthorns School

Music

Music is universal, it makes most people smile.
It reaches all corners of the Earth, mile after mile.
It gathers us together at important times of year,
Birthday, Easter, Christmas, full of joy and cheer.
My sister plays the violin, it sometimes makes me shudder,
But when she eventually gets it right, it makes me want to hug her!
Music's great to dance to, especially rock and pop
And when I listen to Maroon 5, it makes me want to bop!
My grandad likes classical, like Beethoven and Bach.
My family is quite musical and my mum sings in the bath!
Everyone is musical, even if they don't yet know,
Some people tap their fingers, some people click their toes!

Sophie Lock (10)
The Hawthorns School

A Living Hell

Thrice the shark's jaws have left their mark,
Thrice the lion has stalked the dark,
Thrice the wolf has howled at the moon,
The potion's effect will strike at noon.

Fire, fire boil my broth,
Let it flow wild and let it froth.
Show it no mercy and cast my spell,
Give it no kindness, a living hell.

Into the pot goes dead rat's tail,
Swiftly followed by tongue of whale,
Eye of toad and leg of frog,
Mixed together with a pot of smog.

Fire, fire boil my broth,
Let it flow wild and let it froth,
Show it no mercy and cast my spell,
Give it no kindness, a living hell.

Odour of skunk and elephant's tusk,
Stirred together to form a musk,
Venom from a black mamba's bite,
Combined with blood from a fight.

Fire, fire boil my broth,
Let it flow wild and let it froth,
Show it no mercy and cast my spell,
Give it no kindness, a living hell.

Now that the potion is brewed and done,
A dart will be shot from the barrel of a gun,
Suffer the pain and then let it be,
My witch's spell for all to see.

Sam Haydon (10)
The Hawthorns School

Rugby Match

The roar of the crowd
As I approach the pitch
Is thunderous.
I take my position for the start
With enthusiasm inside me
And the game commences.

The whistle for the match to begin
Is blown.
A very tactical restart it taken,
The oval-shaped ball is passed swiftly
Along the line,
Until it gets to me,
Because I run.

As I am sprinting with the ball,
With determination in my face,
Someone is grabbing onto me,
I try to get them off,
But it is as if they are stuck there
With superglue.

I pass the ball
And it reaches my teammate
Who runs and
Plummets down to score a try!

For the last part of the game,
Our tackling is as solid
As a brick wall
And it just so happens,
That we win.

Matthew Rooke (10)
The Hawthorns School

An Otter's Life

Otters swimming all the time
Laying on their backs

Uh-oh, here come the babies
Flapping their tails with glee

Would you want to be
An otter like me?

Swim with me
Eat with me
Do you want to play with me?

Catching fish
Small and large

Swimming in the kelp
Help!

Swim high
Swim low
Do not catch the current's flow.

Rachel Williams (9)
The Hawthorns School

Rugby

'Why do you do it?' said Mum in despair,
'There's mud everywhere, even your hair.'
'I like the teamwork,' I said in reply,
'I like to run and score a try.

There's a guy in our team called Paul,
He passes brilliantly with the ball,
It goes down the line to Clive,
Who gets it on the ground for five.

Taking the conversion for our team,
Fred kicked the ball but missed the beam,
So after the match we went to the club
And after that we went to the pub!'

George Lindley (11)
The Hawthorns School

Chelsea Heroes

Robben's a problem
For the other team.
The only problem with Robben,
He's no problem to me.

Lampard is well hard to me,
He's hard to the other team.
The only thing is,
That he's too hard for me.

Terry's my man of the match,
Captain of the winning team.
He's the man who lifts the Cup,
When we win the League!

Daniel Saunders (8)
The Hawthorns School

My Favourite Day

I can't wait for tomorrow to come
Because my family and I will spend days in the sun
I'm looking forward to lying on the sand
And feeling it run smoothly through my hand

I will make sure I have my bucket and spade
But Mum will make sure we have plenty of shade!

I will look out at the calm sapphire-blue sea
And imagine where the happy dolphins would be

So tomorrow morning we are off on a flight
So I'm off to bed now, night-night.

Charlotte Fagan (8)
The Hawthorns School

Tazzie

I have a dog called Tazzie,
She lives with me at home,
Her fur is coloured black and gold,
She likes to chew a bone!
She comes with me to walk in woods,
In any sort of weather,
She wags her tail to say she's pleased,
When jumping in the heather!
She's my four-legged friend,
Who looks after me,
I couldn't ask for more,
She doesn't do tricks,
But will carry sticks
And if asked, will give you a paw!

Elizabeth Windridge (8)
The Hawthorns School

Golf!

Ball, ball, you're tiny and small,
Smack and you never come back,
Range, range, the club is too strange,
I pick up my bag and go to the flag.

Roll, roll, you fall into the hole,
Green, you're nice and clean,
Tee, tee, it's time for your tea,
I've got a par and I'm off to the car.

Putter, putter, you're as soft as butter,
Click and the ball goes quick,
Wood, wood, I wish I could,
I've won the game and tomorrow I'll do the same.

Euan Hamilton (8)
The Hawthorns School

We Three Witches Round Our Pot

Unicorn's blood and horse's hair,
Dragon's tooth from its bewitched lair.
Eye of howlet, wool of bat,
Stomach of newt and tongue of gnat.

A silvery scale of a fish,
A downtrodden beggar's evil wish.
A sliced and charred puppy dog's tail,
A trapped spectre's screeching wail.

We three witches round our pot,
Deciding what's nice and deciding what's not.
A steaming, bubbling, boiling brew,
That's what we can conjure up for you.

A liver of a strangled snake,
Baby piglet killed at first wake.
A lion's mane, a vulture's wing,
A tiger's stripe and a poisonous bee's sting.

A kitten strangled, steamed and skinned,
A phoenix's feather caught on the wind.
The tough brown hair stolen from a yak,
Now that we're finished, there's no going back.

We three witches round our pot,
Deciding what's nice and deciding what's not.
A steaming, bubbling, boiling brew,
That's what we can conjure up for you.

Katy Barrett (10)
The Hawthorns School

The Beetle, The Ladybird, The Bee And Me

A stag beetle with antlers
On the end of his nose
Was surprised to find
He was wearing clothes

A ladybird had knitted him
A black-spotted jumper
It fitted him well
A little comforter

A happy stag beetle
Walked up the tree
He wanted to show off
His jumper to the bee

The bee was asleep
Buzz, snore, buzz, snore
The beetle climbed up
To the top of the tree

When he got to the top
He shouted so loud
'Come little bee
I am so proud

I have a new jumper
Come see, come see'
But to his surprise
The bee buzzed angrily

Then the little stag beetle
Scuttled down the tree
The bee was behind him
Cross as can be

The beetle hid under
A black-spotted toadstool
The bee couldn't see him
He stood so still

But I could, I found him
I save him from the bee.

David Andrews (8)
The Hawthorns School

Animals In The Kruger

I can see . . .

The rust-coloured impala
graceful, elegant, innocent and serene,
but edgy.
They move around in huge nervous herds
grazing.
The dominant, demented male,
he is strong, forceful and fidgety.
His sharp ears are twitching in the long grass.

The tall, majestic giraffe
striding on its extended, fragile legs.
Its elongated neck sways at every step.
It turns its head above the trees
surveying the savannah.

The gargantuan grey elephant
standing statuesque against the skyline.
He solidly swishes his tail and flaps his large ears
as he curls his snake-like trunk around a branch
and easily pulls it off
as if he was picking daffodils.

The bolshy buffalo
snorts aggressively and stamps her foot.
She tosses her head up and down
and protects her wobbly calf.

The diminutive songololo hurries along
scuttling and scurrying
on its 42 pairs of legs
like a train and its carriages.

Gus Meyer (10)
The Hawthorns School

Dyslexia Oh Drat!

Reading, spelling,
Memory goes blank.
Ordering is wobbly,
Why is English so hard?
Long vowels, short vowels,
Same sounding words,
Where, wear, tail, tale,
But which one to choose?
It's just to confuse.
Why couldn't I have something
I could spell?

It's annoying,
All this . . . toying with words,
At times I knew I would
Be misunderstood,
Which makes me rude.
It gets frustrating,
All this waiting,
For this one thing to end,
When I'm mad,
Mum says, 'Don't be sad.'
But dyslexia doesn't rhyme.

Haig Binnie (9)
The Hawthorns School

The Boggart

Who am I?

I who creeps,
I who hides,
I who slithers where the spider lies.
Who am I?

I the watcher,
The sly one,
The trickster.
Who am I?

I am a changer,
A whisper,
A shifter.
What am I?

I am a learner,
A twister,
An old one.

I am a creature as old as time!

Tom Morris (10)
The Hawthorns School

Hannah

H is for happy and merry,
A is for achiever, talented and smart,
N is for nice and friendly soul,
N is for natural heart of gold,
A is for affectionate, gift from above,
H is for honey, precious and loved.

Hannah Wilkinson (8)
The Hawthorns School

The Gunners

The Gunners play in blue
The Gunners play in red
When they are playing matches
They put their opponents to bed

Arsenal play at Highbury
It's close to Finsbury Park
When they are playing other teams
They always leave their mark

Arsenal are in the Premiership
We are in second place
We're battling Man U and Chelsea
To win the title race

Last year we were champions
We won it at a stroll
Forty-nine games without defeat
We were really on a roll

It looks like Chelsea this year
Are going to win the League
But if we don't win it this time
They'll still be champs to me.

Sam Clark (10)
The Hawthorns School

The Witches Are Here

The wind blows, the witches are here,
The witches are here,
The cats screech, filled with fear!

On their broomsticks, the witches come
Zooming by,
Flying through the summer night sky!

Their long, pointed hats reach out like fingers
Into the night,
Cruel cackles fill the air with fright!

On their broomsticks, ready to cause mischief
And strife,
A blade flashes, is it a knife?

Cos the witches are here,
The witches are here,
The cats screech, filled with fear!

Dominic Turner (8)
The Hawthorns School

His Master's Friend

As quick as a flash
He turned his head
As lightning struck the tree
Around he spun as if on thread
And galloped towards the sea

The waves rolled and crashed
The sky as dark as night
He stumbled on the rocks below
When, suddenly he caught sight
Of his master, the pony's hero.

Isabel Elsey (10)
The Hawthorns School

The Poem

I really wasn't in the mood for doing homework on
                                a Sunday afternoon,
I'd planned my day quite differently.
My PlayStation was calling me, my guitar, the piano,
But Mum said, 'Just sit quietly.'
So I sit here gazing at a blank piece of paper with nothing to write,
I notice a squirrel scampering up a tree in the garden,
One paw on a branch and he's holding it tight.

I keep thinking of things to do in order to put off this chore.
'Mum, I'm hungry, can I look in the fridge?
Can I help you light the fire?
I'm just going to help Dad in the garden.'
But she gives me that look and I know there'll be trouble in store.

My mind has gone completely blank, every thought has flown away,
What am I going to write a poem about? How can I make it
                                last for 30 lines?
Shall I write about the cat? Space monsters?
                        Skateboarding? Christmas?
I know, I think I'll make a paper aeroplane, that should
                                waste some more time.

I've run out of excuses now and I'm starting to get worried,
This blank sheet of paper is still inviting me to write,
The story of a boy who had a problem with his homework,
Now all the things he did to put it off have taken flight.

Gabriel Gould-Davies (9)
The Hawthorns School

Irish Rugby

There were fifteen men dressed in green,
Who made up the Irish team.
Their captain was Brian O'Driscoll,
Who tackled right up to the whistle
And dared to pursue his dream.

They recently won the Triple Crown,
Causing delight in Dublin Town.
They beat England, Scotland and Wales,
In blustery winds and gales,
Leaving the rest sad and down.

Anthony Foley and Keith Wood
Are both extremely good.
Two of the best that Ireland have had,
They both went to school with my dad.
A Grand Slam this year would be good!

Sean Addley (9)
The Hawthorns School

Baby Rory

My baby brother is as cute as can be,
He is warm and soft and very cuddly.

He has ten tiny fingers and ten tiny toes,
Bright blue eyes and a cute button nose.

I really love my brother, even though he is very smelly,
I even love him when he is crying and I cannot hear the telly.

Oliver Kerr (8)
The Hawthorns School

Winter Vineyard

Row upon row
Line upon line
Field upon field
Of gnarled old vines

Wooden posts support their legs
Wires support their arms
Like old men standing in lines
Only kissed by the deer
For their juicy buds

Clipped right back they are
Naked in the wind and wet
With peeling skin and stubby hair

And with every October
They are robbed of their sweet green grapes
Their only pride
Then they mourn till the next bunch comes
And are mocked by the grass which is always green.

Max Baart (10)
The Hawthorns School

The Dragon Slayer

The dragon flew into the night,
Peering down for a worthy fight,
The slayer mounted his eagle steed
And looked around for a person in need,
Then he saw the dragon up high
And soared into the pitch-black sky,
The dragon crouched ready to fight
And the slayer glided past the starlit night.

Kitty Marryat (8)
The Hawthorns School

My Wish

Rushing here, rushing there,
Snow spinning through the air,
Sledges sliding round the bend,
Shouts of 'hike' and 'low'.

Soft fluffy fur,
Shiny noses, chomping jaws,
Special shoes for frozen paws,
Tails waving madly.

Orange, brown, black, grey,
Which do I like best?
Barking, yapping through work and play,
Trained well, ready for the day.

I love them a lot,
I wish I had a husky.

Katherine Perkins (10)
The Hawthorns School

My Pets

Here's my dog,
Her name is Mog,
She dances around,
She's so sweet,
But she always wants something to eat!

Here's my pony,
His name's Tony,
He runs fast,
But he finishes last!

Here's my cat,
His name is Matt,
He's so fat,
But he's still my cat!

Charlie Bramhall (9)
The Hawthorns School

My Family

There's me. Yeah me.
I love fashion,
Lipstick, blush and mascara.
There's also my two bunnies,
Poppy and Misty.

Then there's Dad,
Nearly always sleeping,
Or working -
Sometimes cooking,
Really stinky breath.

Then there's Mum,
So practical,
Very fussy,
Everything has to be done perfectly,
'Put effort into everything you do.'

Then there's Gideon, my brother, my little brother,
Such a runny nose,
Always on the football pitch,
Kicking a football round everything,
Rubbing out every wrong spelling.

Then there's Ffion, she's my little sister,
Always sucking her thumb,
Always with her blanky,
Dancing, swirling and skipping,
She dances nearly every day.

So there's my family,
There's me, my dad, my mum,
Also my little brother and my little sister.
All different,
But there we are,
We were all made to be different.

Abi Haffenden (9)
The Hawthorns School

My Sister

My sister goes to a grammar school,
She's pretty, tough and tall,
She has brown eyes
And muscley thighs,
I love her lots and lots.

She likes to play sport,
She's always last to leave the court,
She likes to do art
And she's a bit smart,
Her favourite sport is hockey!

She's very kind,
She has an imaginative mind
And her room is a bit of a mess,
Occasionally she can be a pest,
But usually, she's nice.

If you need a sister, mine's the one you want,
Because she is number 1!
And she's extremely fun,
But tough luck, she's mine
And this is the last line!

Georgia Paul (9)
The Hawthorns School

Me!

This poem is about me,
Leave it be or come and see.
I have bright, rosy cheeks,
That help me through the weeks.
If I am ever down,
My eyes go brown,
But they change colour into greens and blues
And get all sticky when I'm using the glue.
I have lots of really good friends
And we can have arguments but it soon ends.
I have such a lovely mum and dad,
But sometimes I get very sad.
I always like to hide my tears,
And my dad likes to have some beers,
He normally shouts out, 'Hey, cheers!'
I do not have a lot to say,
It's the end of my poem, 'Hip hip hooray!'

Rosie Meade (10)
The Hawthorns School

My Mind

My mind is a wonderful place;
There are blue and red bees and funny-shaped trees,
There's a rocket-powered ship
Made of strawberry whip,
There's a sea creature, yellow and white
Which is very bright,
There is a hill with a house on top,
Which is shaped like a mop,
There's a flower bigger than the Eiffel Tower,
There's grass as green as it can get,
There is world peace and my niece
And there're parts which I dare not share,
Not even with myself.

Thomas Paul (11)
The Hawthorns School

Swim Race

As I approach the starting line
My heart starts thumping madly
I try to calm myself down so
That I don't swim really badly

As I dive into the water
I feel it rushing past my face
It feels like a warm, creamy blanket
As I try to win the race

I feel myself crashing through the water
As fast as I can go
And I hope the other swimmers
Are very, very slow

When I am in the water
I can hear the crowd scream my name
And I swim even harder
Towards the end of my lane

When I get to the end
I know I've kept my pace
Because the crowd shouts my name
As I win the final race!

Emily McCarthy (9)
The Hawthorns School

Winter

W inter is the coldest part of the year.
 I n winter, there is sometimes snow.
N early always there is rain.
T ry to wear warm clothing in winter or you will be very cold.
E arly evening, it gets very dark.
R oasting hot fires keep us warm.

Michael Stephen (9)
The Hawthorns School

Bronze Owl - You're Special To Me

I tried hard at geography,
I tried hard at PE,
I tried hard at maths,
I tried hard at DT.

It was in history and English and swimming that I did well,
I went to the head and he said I did swell.
I felt honoured, excited, fantastic and proud,
'I now have four head's copies,' I shouted aloud!

It was at assembly that I realised,
It was all worth it in the end,
When I was called up and presented with my
Miniature new friend.

Dark and shiny, with feathers engraved all around,
Upright he is perched, wise without a sound,
He was pinned to my sweater,
I looked at him with glee,
Little bronze owl, you're so special to me.

Alexandro Zaccarini (9)
The Hawthorns School

My Pet

My pet is very shy and never looks me in the eye.
She never wants to come out to play and only wants to hide away.
She spends all day in her house, anyone would think
        she was a mouse.
She sits alone in her tube and watches me while I play my flute.
My beautiful pet is brown and creamy-white and only runs
         around at night.
She is very soft and fluffy and her cheeks sometimes go puffy.
At night, she will run upon her red and yellow wheel
And in the morning she will eat her meal.
Who is my pet? Do you know?

Charlotte Morris (9)
The Hawthorns School

Seasons

Summer
Summer is warm,
Time for a storm,
Flowers grow,
Rivers flow.

Autumn
Leaves are falling,
Weather's appalling,
Conkers found,
Covering the ground.

Winter
Snow is everywhere,
Trees stand cold and bare,
Christmas drawing near,
The season of good cheer.

Spring
Lambs frolic and play,
In the bright spring day,
Flowers sway to and fro,
Streams begin to flow.

Susannah Pike (8)
The Hawthorns School

The Truth About Fairies

The magical, mystical figures,
With sparkly, diamond
And ruby dresses that are
Luscious lilac.
On their feet are
Glittery ballet shoes,
They wear crowns
Which are silver and crystal.
Their hair is soft and flowing,
It is tied neatly in a bun.
They sit beautifully by
A rosebush,
Their legs curved,
Arms resting on their legs,
In the position of a mermaid.
Their figures are petite and thin,
Their attitude
Kind, sweet, loving
And sometimes shy.
They only come around at night
And fly around my room,
Spreading sparkles around and over me.
In the day, they play sweetly with their friends
And have eight hours sleep as well,
They smell like lavender strips and pot pourrie,
I can hear their wings fluttering,
I believe in fairies and these are some
Of the wonderful things about them!

Imogen Tantam (9)
The Hawthorns School

Boogie

I don't like swimming
I don't like singing
But the thing that works for me is dancing
People say I am good, so I believe them
I like disco dancing
I can boogie to the floor when it's the mad March disco
I go mad like they tell me to
I always start the conga and the can-can
People copy my moves
So why don't they build me my own stage?
I actually thing they should make me my own TV show
I know, I'll ask my mum
Hopefully she'll say yes
If she does, I'll be famous
And you know that Britney Spears girl
Well, she gets all the wrong moves
And that girl
What's her name?
Oh yes, Emma Bunton
I ask my mum and she says no
Well, maybe I should start ballroom dancing.

Ellen McLaren (8)
The Hawthorns School

Feelings

I am feeling very confused,
I don't know what I'm doing.
I'm singing in the school concert,
At which children are booing!
I am now very sad,
Because I feel alone.
As if I'm not wanted,
As if I'm not known.
But there's one person in the audience,
Who's not laughing at all.
I can't see him that well,
Because he's very small.
That person is my friend,
He's trying to support me.
That makes me feel warm inside,
Which I think means I'm happy.

Jamie Oyebode (10)
The Hawthorns School

School

I see the teachers going red in the face,
I see the pupils, sitting at their place,
I see the birds having a flying race.

I hear the keyboards tapping,
I hear the teachers napping,
I hear all the birds flapping.

I feel happy to see a friend,
I feel the past is at an end,
I feel there are animals to tend.

I hope this gets another drive,
I hope Year 6 is as good as 5,
I hope the creatures stay alive.

Matthew Pollard (10)
The Hawthorns School

Crystal Palace FC

I hear the thundering feet of the Palace fans
Going up to the Arthur Wait stand
It is Saturday afternoon at Selhurst Park
Andy Johnson and his designer penalties
Scores with ease from 40 feet
It is Saturday afternoon at Selhurst Park
Wayne Routledge and his supreme foot skills
Comes from the side to fool the goalkeeper in style
It is Saturday afternoon at Selhurst Park

They are the Eagles but, like a cat, they have 9 lives
They come back when they are down
They are as strong as wild elephants
They are battling up the Barclay's Premiership
They will succeed
Hooray for Palace!

Michael Sheldrake (8)
The Hawthorns School

Skiing

A figure stands upon a weary white mountain slope,
Behind a crystal-blue sky, cloudless and bright.
As he twists and turns on this special land,
The snow is fresh and as white as white.
Now as his journey continues, the danger warns,
A fresh new glacier appears with the birth of a new dawn.

Charlie Dockery (9)
The Hawthorns School

The Amazing Turtle

The amazing turtle
Is an absolutely great fact,
He sits on the sand
With a long top hat.

He grabs all the balls
And hides them somewhere,
Some tourists run away,
Some tourists stare.

He's allergic to water,
His favourite thing is sand,
Fortunately he knows the beach
Like the back of his hand.

Fifteen years after his birth,
His mother popped up and said,
'Get down to Earth, it's a lot better to have a swim
Than to be stared at by him.

You look stupid in that top hat that you wear.'
'Oh, that's why all the people stare.'

The amazing turtle
Put one toe in the water,
Then he thought, *I shouldn't oughta*,
Then he thought, *I won't die*,
So he dived in and had a try.

Then he jumped out of the sea with glee,
When he knew he was absolutely free
From the people, free from the sand,
Free from the umbrellas stuck in the ground.

Jacob Holme (9)
The Hawthorns School

My Mr Softy

Mr Softy, white as snow
I like to groom him to make him glow
Sometimes as we ride, he goes fast
I love him so much, he's such a sweet fellow

Softy is very kind to me, with friends of mine
We like to play games if we have time
His jumping is not great, he does try
He sometimes would prefer decline

When I call him in for tea at the end of the day
He gallops all the way to me for his hay
Softy loves his feed at night
His stable is soft, yellow where he will stay

Softy is my best pony friend of all
I know he is only so very small
Whilst I'm seven, he is fine for me
Sooner than I would like, I will be much too tall.

Hannah Martin (7)
The Hawthorns School

Excitement Is . . .

Excitement is . . . an adventure film.
Excitement is . . . being a football star.
Excitement is . . . *dazzling!*
Excitement is . . . travelling far.
Excitement is . . . joyfulness.
Excitement is . . . tummy-spinning.
Excitement is . . . *heart-hammering.*
Excitement is . . . mouth-grinning.

Alfie Edwards (9)
The Mount Primary School

Newborn Nephew

It was Christmas Day
And I went to my brother, Jason's house,
He called me into the kitchen,
Showed me a scan,
Black and grey, lines and dots
And the baby . . .
Laying down, curved like a banana.
At first Kelly looked . . .
Normal.
The next time I saw her,
Her stomach was bigger,
She looked like she'd eaten
Too many chocolates.
Then, as time went by,
As though she'd swallowed a watermelon . . .
Whole!
And finally,
When she looked like
She was going to burst,
I made a phone call to my brother
And was told:
'Kelly's having the baby right this minute!'
I first saw him
When he was seven days old,
All cosy and warm in his yellow and white babygrow.
He smelt baby-sweet,
He cried and smiled
And curled his fingers,
His name is Jimmy
And he looks like an angel.

Elizabeth O'Connell (10)
The Mount Primary School

The Bully

I was walking out from school
And she was waiting for me,
I tried to run,
But she caught up with me.

'What should I do?'
I ask myself at night.
I can't tell my mum or my teachers
Of my horrible fright.

But then one day,
Fed up with feeling deserted,
I told my teacher
And the problem was sorted.

When she goes past,
I'm sometimes scared,
So I start to run fast . . .
She just *stares*.

Bethany Russell (10)
The Mount Primary School

My Friend Because . . .

She's my friend because . . .
She helps me,
Talks with me,
Has fun with me,
Plays with me,
Shares jokes with me,
Explains English to me
When I don't understand everything
Because I'm Polish,
She is a good companion,
Is honest with me
And never breaks up with me.

Angelika Molas (8)
The Mount Primary School

Life In Morocco

Brown dust blows
When the wind hits it around
The diminutive mountains
In the distance.
Wild dogs without owners
Howl in the evening
And search for rabbits
In the greenlands.
Chickens with little chicks
Run around the garden
And night crickets whisper.
Donkeys wear black crosses
On their backs
Imposed there by God
So they are protected
From harm.
Rattling, ragged, smashed-up, dusty cars
Make a booming noise
As wheels hit the holes in the road
And get damaged.
The sky turns scarlet at dawn
And in the morning
The sun is like
A red snooker ball
In the sky.

Imad Sahara (10)
The Mount Primary School

Leaving Home

I left Iraq when
I was eight years old.
We packed our bags
And began an interminable voyage.
The distress and worry
Was like a devil around me,
Shielding me from the outside world
And suffocating me
With sadness and terror.
The sky, tangerine and scarlet,
Sand and stones hurtling past us,
Hitting our car like bullets from a machine gun.
But there were no guns at all.
Only . . .
The nightmare *did* arrive,
When I was hundreds of miles away,
Safe and sound,
In a new peaceful world.
But still . . .
Fire and war, swelling the country,
Killing people
And making a murderous meal
For the Grim Reaper.

Ali Kokaz (11)
The Mount Primary School

Summer Sights

Summer sunshine
Keeps me blazing
Coconut trees
Shade me
Birds flutter
Through the sky
Swimming pools
Cool me
Beautiful butterflies
Hover over flowers
Velvety bees
Buzz dreamily
An amazing sunset
On the landscape
Makes me
Feel sleepy.

Rebekah Longley (9)
The Mount Primary School

I Love Art

I love art
It makes me feel ecstatic
It ignites my day
It can make my heart
Fill with sorrow
Satisfaction and joy
It can sweep
Away my troubles
And make me feel soothed
The colours make me want
To scream and shout
To cry and smile
To dance and prance
I want to share my happiness
With the world.

Sophie Eamer (10)
The Mount Primary School

Summer Sounds

Voice of bird,
Whistling to me.

Butterfly wings,
Swishing delicately.

Croaking frogs,
Leaping gracefully.

Lazy crickets,
Clicking rhythmically.

Bandstand orchestra,
Serenading me.

Dancing trees,
Dance to me

And let me
Do that too.

Kelly Neves (10)
The Mount Primary School

Unwanted

The bully is a persecutor,
The bully is a push-around.

The bully makes me frightened,
The bully makes me feel rejected.

The bully is a hassler,
The bully is a harasser.

The bully makes me feel left out,
The bully makes me broken-hearted.

The bully makes terror twist in my tummy,
I'm glad we helped the bully to stop.

Victoria Westlake (8)
The Mount Primary School

The Greatest Mum In The World

There's only one
Like my mum,
She's the best,
Better than the rest.
Whenever I'm sad,
She makes me happy,
Whenever I'm bad,
She doesn't get mad,
But helps to
Calm me down
And make it better.
She's always fair,
When we're being unfair.
She tries to repair
The tears that
Rip us up
And make us quarrel.
She shows us
She loves us,
In too many ways
To say
And I love her,
Beyond the horizon,
More than she will
Ever know.

Sian Hughes (9)
The Mount Primary School

Beautiful World

Dazzling moon,
Shine in the water.
Bare trees,
Blanket the sky
With your
1,000-year-old branches.
Biting winds,
Freeze my enemies
With your
Chomping coldness.
Golden stars,
Decorate me
With your
Shining magnificence
And greatness
Of light.

Ian Kincaid (10)
The Mount Primary School

Hello Friend

Loneliness ender,
Joy sender,
Best cuddler,
Love hugger,
Game player,
Song singer,
Happy smiler,
Secret sharer,
Talk together
'Duck-duck gooser',
Hand holder,
Welcome to
Our playground!

Anijet Chaudhry (10) & Dina Abrev (8)
The Mount Primary School

No Room

You're a
Heartbreaker
Tear-maker
Arm-puncher
Jumper-puller
Skin-pincher
Face-smacker
Bossy-booter
Ball-stealer
Bad-word-sayer
Lie-teller
Misery-seller
And there's no room
For you in our school,
Goodbye.

Azra Mohamedali Abbas & Miriam Khaled (8)
The Mount Primary School

Kennings

Spine chilling
Heart freezing
Bone biting
Bad speaking
Tear flooding
Fun killing
Heart breaking
Respect changing
Bitter terror
Fear bringing

A: A bully.

Rhiannon Lewis (9)
The Mount Primary School

Kennings

Metal clanging
Cars crashing
Plates smashing
Dogs howling
Trains colliding
Nail scraping
Ear piercing
Cat screeching
Glass breaking
Fireworks exploding
Deafening screaming
Earthquakes erupting
Loud shouting
Rule flouting

How the bully makes me feel.

Zoe Wolff (8)
The Mount Primary School

Autumn Morning

Owls hoot peacefully
Fog hangs lightly
Wind blows calmly
Rain drops gently
Robins sing sweetly
Daddy-long-legs moves crazily
Geese fly anxiously
Milkman shivers coldly
Children wake up slowly
Eat breakfast quickly
Get dressed hurriedly
School starts suddenly
Children play nicely
Cat walks swiftly.

Grace Roberts (8)
The Mount Primary School

Helping

My friend was being bullied,
It made me upset,
I didn't like it.
I tried to talk
To the bully,
To sort it out,
But in the end
We told
The teacher.
She listened
And suddenly,
Everything got better.

Rose Kincaid (8)
The Mount Primary School

Magical Journey

The luminous moon,
Sparkles on the water
And bare trees,
Camouflage me.
The biting winds
Masticate me.
Golden stars
Sprinkle magical,
Glowing, spellbinding
Shapes through my path,
Into the dark,
Living, winter forest.

Pragash Rasalingham (10)
The Mount Primary School

I Want A World Without Bullies

I have a friend
Who tells me
Not to play with
Children from
Another religion
If I play with them
He is not my friend
He makes me
Feel bullied
He tries to get me
Into trouble
If I'm not
His friend
Sometimes . . .
I cry.

Davinder Tal (8)
The Mount Primary School

Fading Away

They had been
my friends before.
Suddenly, they
acted like
they hadn't been.
They started to
threaten me.
I felt like
I was
fading away
from
everything
and
everyone.

Monu Sachdeva (8)
The Mount Primary School

My Special Friend

She's my friend because
She makes me laugh
She's fun-bringing
She tells good jokes
And makes me happy
I can trust her
With my secrets
Because I know
She won't tell
She is forever fair
And when we
Are together
I feel like
I have been
Sprinkled with
Magic!

Hersimran Kaur (9)
The Mount Primary School

Don't Stand For . . .

Bullies being horrible
Unpleasant words
Being spoken
Lonely and lying bullies
Ignorant, yelling persecutors
Giggling horribly
In the playground

Tell the teacher
And
Stop them!

Nicole McDonell (8)
The Mount Primary School

Happiness

Happiness is a birthday
and blowing out candles.

Happiness is the smell
of a bunch of ruby roses.

Happiness is having friends
to smile with.

Happiness is dancing
with feet like fireflies.

Happiness is pasta
with tomato sauce.

Happiness is painting
flowers in an art lesson.

Zahrah Vencatasamy (8)
The Mount Primary School

Happiness Is . . .

Happiness is having friends
to share secrets with.
Happiness is caring
and making people feel noticed.
Happiness is being with family
and feeling protected.
Happiness is lots of sweets
but no rotting teeth.
Happiness is singing
out loud in the shower.
Happiness is love.
It makes your heart
feel *big!*

Hollie Fouracre (8)
The Mount Primary School

Danger

Danger is
fast cars.
Danger is
flying darts.
Danger is
gigantic sharks.
Danger is
stopping hearts.
Danger is
leaping sparks.
Danger is
alone in the dark.
Danger is
fierce barks.
Danger is
druggy parks.

Sam Besant (10)
The Mount Primary School

Advice To A Friend

P lay with us
E ven when you're sad
A lways talk to us
C aring for each other
E very day.

Callum Russell (8)
The Mount Primary School

Fear Is . . .

Fear is
Darkness.
Fear is
Being alone.
Fear is
Sadness.
Fear is
A gloomy fog.
Fear is
Goosebumps.
Fear is
A graveyard.
Fear is
A
Shiver
Down
My
Spine!

Usamah Essenouni (9)
The Mount Primary School